Death of Dignity

Death of Dignity
Angola's Civil War

Victoria Brittain

Pluto Press
LONDON • CHICAGO, ILLINOIS

First published in 1998 by Pluto Press
345 Archway Road, London N6 5AA

British Library Cataloguing-in-Publication Data
A catalogue record for this book is available from the British Library

ISBN 0 7453 1252 7 hbk

Designed and produced for Pluto Press by
Chase Production Services, Chadlington, OX7 3LN
Typeset from disk by Stanford DTP Services, Northampton
Printed in the EC by TJ International, Padstow

Contents

Acknowledgements

With warmest thanks for my home from home in Luanda to Ruth and Lucio, and to Liz. Without their constant friendship and support I would not have had the strength to look at many painful things in Angola. I am grateful too to many other Angolans who generously gave me their time and hospitality over and over again. My thanks for help with the otherwise insurmountable difficulties of transport and logistics go to Save the Children, the World Food Programme, UNDP, Oxfam and Norwegian People's Aid; for help with the text to Marga. Augusta was my indomitable companion on many trips, and Thea constantly encouraged me to stop thinking about the breaking of Angola and write it down.

A Note on Sources

This book comes out of more than ten years of visits to Angola, from 1984 to 1996. The official documents of the period, and the memoirs of some key protagonists, tell only a bland version of the story. During those tumultuous years of power struggles between Unita's backer, apartheid South Africa, aided by the United States, and an Angolan leadership ready to do almost anything for peace, I was a witness to many private discussions on the Angolan side. It was a time of secrets, a time of polarisation and taking sides, with no middle way for impartial observers. The small intellectual elite in Luanda is like a village: everyone knows each other, alliances, betrayals, a rise or fall in the power structure, are common knowledge. Friendships grew over the years in the intensity of this hothouse. My sources are therefore mostly anonymous. What these Angolans told me, which allowed me to understand the ruthlessness with which their country's hopes were crushed, came not in interviews, but in long private conversations often over days of travelling, visiting remote towns and villages where the war's terrible toll was plain on every face. Unita's Jonas Savimbi made a Faustian pact with some of the most powerful countries in the world which brought his country to the brink of destruction and ruined the lives of untold tens of thousands of peasants. I have interviewed too many of them and seen too much of their suffering to listen to the lying justifications of those responsible, so there are no interviews here with Unita officials, though many hours of listening to Unita defectors has fed into my ideas about that organisation. Nor are there interviews with Western diplomats, the normal staple fare of Western journalists – most of them were content to pretend to, or talk themselves into, an impartiality which obscured the truth of the horror that happened here. As the situation swung from war to an uneasy peace in 1991 and back to war within 15 months, Angola became peopled with foreigners in powerful positions. It was tragic that so many of them had astonishingly little grasp of the history of violence distorted by a decade and a half of skilful propaganda by the Americans and South Africans who allied themselves with Savimbi's primitive fascism. Many of these new foreigners in the UN and the aid agencies, in their turn, helped to normalise that grim option for Angola.

PREFACE

Men who made a revolution, and watched it taken from them

Arriving in Luanda from Europe for the first time in late 1984, the airport was an instant warning that this was a world where people lived by other codes far from my experience. It was stifling hot in the crowd pushing towards immigration, mosquitoes buzzed and bit, and it was completely dark at the entrance to the terminal, the only light far ahead behind the high screens of the immigration officials. I knew no one in Angola and spoke not a word of Portuguese. In the hour or so of squeezing towards the desk, falling progressively further and further to the back of the crowd, I had plenty of time to regret the curiosity which had driven me through the laborious process of getting a rare journalist's visa and now appeared to promise two weeks completely out of my depth. Suddenly, years of working in Uganda after Idi Amin when the entire infrastructure had collapsed and journalists had to travel with their own food and petrol, Sudan when it was overwhelmed with tens of thousands of Ugandan and Ethiopian refugees, Somalia during the war with Ethiopia, or the Sahel of the great drought which destroyed the centuries-old nomadic civilisation of a whole region of West Africa, seemed a poor preparation for the toughness of Angola. Waiting in the dark, the heat and the crush, I went over the little I knew about Angola's war, and the stubborn determination to try to understand it which lay behind this visit.

Since Angola's independence from Portugal in 1975, South Africa had repeatedly invaded and occupied the southern provinces. A camp of Swapo refugees, including many children, had been massacred from South African helicopter gun ships at Kassinga, an ANC teacher at the University of Lubango, Jeanette Schoon, and her small daughter had been assassinated by a South African letter bomb, tens of thousands of peasants had been killed, kidnapped or driven from their villages by land mines – victims of Unita terror tactics. President dos Santos had recently put the cost of destruction since independence at $10 billion. All this I knew only second hand from piecing together scraps of news out of one of the most closed countries in Africa. It added up to catastrophe, but it was a catastrophe out of sight, visited upon anonymous people whose pain

viii

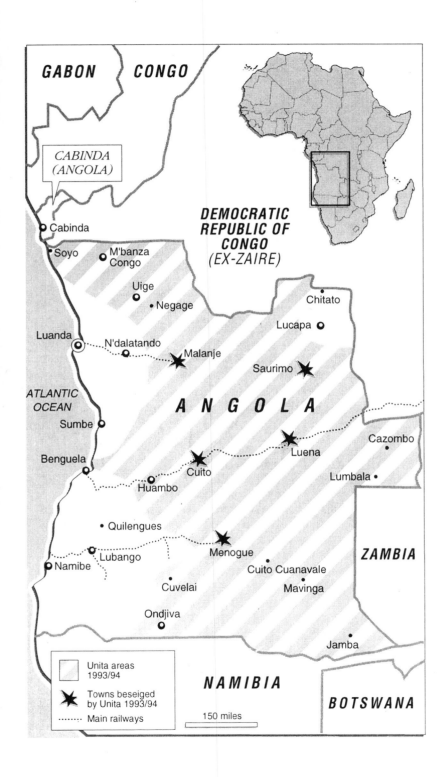

GABON

CONGO

CABINDA
(ANGOLA)

○ Cabinda

• Soyo   ○ M'banza
           Congo

DEMOCRATIC
REPUBLIC OF
CONGO
(EX-ZAIRE)

Uige
○
• Negage

• Chitato

Lucapa ○

Luanda
◎   N'dalatando
           ○
              • Malanje

Saurimo ★

ANGOLA

ATLANTIC
OCEAN

Sumbe ○

Cazombo
•

★
Luena

Benguela
○
           ★
           Cuito
      ○
      Huambo

Lumbala •

• Quilengues

○
Lubango
○ Namibe

★
Menogue

ZAMBIA

•
Cuito Cuanavale
•
Mavinga

• Cuvelai

Ondjiva
○

•
Jamba

Unita areas
1993/94

★ Towns beseiged
    by Unita 1993/94

••••••• Main railways

NAMIBIA

BOTSWANA

150 miles

never impinged on the rest of the world. Unlike Africa's better known disasters – famines, coups, border wars – which hit the headlines and the television screens for a week or a month, Angola's disaster had gone on for so many years that it was no longer news. It triggered no outrage nor even much interest.

My visa had come with an invitation from the Angolan Women's Organisation (OMA). South Africa's ten-year-old undeclared war with Angola had the country on its knees and the Angolan authorities were deeply sceptical about Western journalists, who mostly reported Angola out of Johannesburg or through interviews with the fluent and media-friendly leader of Unita, Jonas Savimbi, at his headquarters in southeast Angola under the vigilant protection of the South African military, and none were allowed in except with a programme carefully controlled by the authorities. The relief at finally being met in the darkness outside the terminal by a woman from OMA was so extreme that neither her minimal English nor the nastiness of my stuffy room on the tenth floor of a shabby hotel mattered that night.

But 24 hours later I was in despair as I saw how little I was likely to find out or understand in this place to which I lacked any key. The hotel was state owned and mostly used then by foreigners from socialist countries working here in Angola as teachers, doctors, engineers or military advisers. The lady from OMA gave me vouchers which allowed me to eat in the down-at-heel restaurant on the twentieth floor reached by one small lift which worked only intermittently. A slow procession went up and down the narrow staircase for half an hour either side of the meal hours. The restaurant was filled with tables crowded with groups of chattering Cubans, East Europeans, Vietnamese, Chinese and Angolans. I sat alone and no one spoke to me. Beyond the language barrier was the even bigger one that I, apparently alone in the hotel and probably, I felt, in the whole country, was not part of the common fight by these tough people for the survival of Angola's independence. The meals were torture, not just because the food was hard to swallow, though it certainly was, but because I would stare at the faces and imagine the dramas of their experiences, their stories, their thoughts, and know I would never know them.

Once a day my minder from OMA took me out to a formal interview with a selected government official or to an OMA project where the women of a poor barrio sang and danced for a visitor. It was a paradox that while the single party, the Popular Movement for the Liberation of Angola (MPLA), or its offshoot OMA in my case, could organise entry into anything or a meeting with anybody, lack of imagination and flexibility meant they chose to organise my seeing things only at the superficial level of a prepared presentation. And I was too ignorant and too embarrassed by my ignorance to force a change in the agenda. The formality of these encounters as much as the language barrier again meant the frustration of seeing these people living through the drama of war, upheaval, dispossession, bereavement and poverty, as though on the other side of a frosted glass pane. Because the realities were not articulated in any normally casual conversation I felt I was not grasping them, but merely becoming overwhelmed by a crushing sensation of the pain and injustice which underlay all these individual experiences.

There were flashes of something different. I had asked to see the Air Force Commander, Iko Carreira, a hero of the liberation war and a friend of one of my friends in Europe. There was no formality and no interpreters for the interview in his office in the Ministry of Defence. Sophisticated, amusing and extremely good looking, Iko was immediately friendly and prepared to spend hours on the ABC of the current military situation and to explain where Unita were pushing forward. Confident and optimistic, he went on to spell out their dependence on South Africa, and the illegal use of Namibia by the South African military, and to forecast that once Namibia was independent Unita would lose its lifeline and be easily defeated. He pointed to the maps on the wall and drew a line showing where the South African military were still occupying a stretch of the south of the country. Then, very casually, he gave me my first taste of how personally things get done in Angola. 'I'll get a plane to fly you down there before you leave and you can see for yourself they're still there, months after agreeing to leave.' No formal request would ever have produced such a gift of firsthand experience, but Iko did it and I did not see him again to thank him.

I used to stand on a chair in the hotel to look out of my bedroom window at a small slice of Luanda. Broken pavements, pot-holed roads, huge piles of rubbish, empty shop windows, crumbling apartment blocks were a desolate background to the glimpse of the beautiful, long, curved bay which is the capital's focus. Palm trees against the blue water and a fringe of sand on the far side of the bay were like a hint of a normal West African coastal world. In contrast, on the streets downtown the people showed clearly the strain of a society disrupted by war. Country women in faded wraparound cloths with babies tied on their backs, young people in the rather flash styles of downtown Lisbon, and ex-soldiers in tattered uniforms and usually on crutches, made their way wearily. Neither the sacked and looted towns of Uganda after Idi Amin in 1979, nor the dilapidated hotels and run-down streets of Accra in 1982 after Flight Lieutenant Rawlings staged his second take-over, gave off the atmosphere of overwhelming melancholy of Luanda in the mid-1980s. Here the faces were set, hard to look at.

But one evening, picking my way with a torch between the garbage and the pot-holes among apartment blocks whose numbers were chalked at random, to find a friend of a friend said to live on the eighth floor, I began to find an exhilaration beyond the melancholy. Here were people whose matter-of-fact acceptance of an everyday life lived against the background of rare electricity, sporadic water supply, no telephone, no public transport, and all the shortages of a war economy, plus its sudden deaths from the continuing invasions and sabotage by South Africa, had a resilience beyond my experience. My friend's friends were part of the mainly white and mestiço intellectual circle of Luanda which had opposed Portuguese colonialism and supported the MPLA. These people had often become ministers, ambassadors or other key officials in the early, exciting years of independence that had now vanished as the new war gripped the country. The evening's conversation ranged from French movies to Algerian politics via American culture. Everyone there spoke French and some English – I was released from my prison of non-communication, though no one seemed to want to talk much about Angola.

Other evenings in Luanda in other flats of friends of friends, painstakingly found by tramping round with my torch, ignoring the rats, brought me more of these cultivated, engaging people, but still no real clues about Angola. I was beginning to learn that, as I had felt so overwhelmingly at the dark airport, this was not a society which worked by normal rules, nor which had much coherence. For one thing there seemed to be little overlap between the formality and rigidity of the MPLA – the Party, the country's defence against the onslaught from South Africa – and these agreeable, sophisticated people in the capital.

I had asked in my original formal visa application to go to Huambo, provincial capital of the Central Highlands and now an island of government control surrounded by areas where Unita held sway. My minder from OMA got the tickets after several fruitless trips to Angolan Airlines, long waits in queues which never moved and several cancellations of the departure date. The airport in Luanda was a different kind of shock this time. After a long wait for a much-delayed flight there was a sudden rush as of a football crowd to the steps of the plane. The OMA lady proved to have sharp elbows and to be a determined fighter and pushed me through the crowd and on to the plane with extraordinary force. People stood aside politely for a foreigner. Several hundred weary-looking people, laden down with bags and children, were left behind on the tarmac, disconsolately heading back to the hard benches of the departure area to wait for another flight, another day.

If Luanda was melancholy, Huambo was desolate. The plane circled abruptly down to avoid Unita missiles, leaving stomachs behind with a lurch. The airport was a windy strip with dilapidated buildings and a tattered MPLA flag flying. The streets were even more broken down than those of the capital, shops closed, apartment blocks crumbling, offices empty. Tangled bushes of dusty bougainvillaea sprayed orange, purple and red flowers out across cracked pavements, the few vehicles on the roads seemed to be all military trucks. The sound of tapping crutches filled the silence, empty trouser legs flapped below the faces of soldiers so young-looking that the blankness of their eyes was impossible to meet without feeling you were intruding. Huambo was raw pain. It was the town which hooked me and ensured that Angola's tragedy would always be refracted to me at a special angle.

The town was under virtual siege by Unita and could be reached only by the irregular internal flight we had come on. The electricity and water supplies had been sabotaged, the railway from the coast was closed after repeated ambushes by Unita and stretches of the track being blown up. The Benguela railway was a key target for Unita and had suffered an estimated $60 million worth of damage from repeated sabotage. The town's factories stood empty. That night, in another hotel room just as dark and grim as that in Luanda, explosions and gunfire punctuated the darkness and made it impossible to sleep. In contrast with Luanda the highland air was cold, there was a bitter wind and it began to rain.

Miete Marcelino, head of OMA in Huambo, picked me up in her car the next morning and showed me around a day care centre, the hospital and, with an escort of two trucks of soldiers, one in front of the car and one behind, an orphanage a few miles outside the town. It was an empty shelter where the children were fed and sheltered, nothing beyond the barest necessities. On the way we passed a makeshift camp on the edge of town of thousands of displaced peasants. By mid-afternoon we reached the hospital where a new crop of mine victims lay on iron bedsteads with no mattresses, faces stunned by shock and agony. Angolan, Cuban and Russian doctors passed in and out of the operating room where the amputations were being carried out, drawn with the exhaustion of working round the clock with minimal resources. Miete Marcelino leaned over the cot of a skeletal child with marasmus, who an Angolan nurse told us had little chance of surviving, and touched his mother's hand with sympathy. It seemed as though all Huambo's pain was concentrated in that tiny, shrivelled face of an innocent victim. (Ten years later, visiting that hospital in a different era, an Angolan doctor with a deeply lined, gentle face came up and reminded me that he had taken us round that day. 'You were in an OMA delegation and you cried over one child who was dying ... all of us had long before given up crying.')

Miete Marcelino, tall, slim, the mother of seven children, asked me to spend the evening with her family instead of going back to the terrible silence and cold of the hotel. It was a welcome escape from confronting my thoughts about what I had seen of shattered lives in that one day. Miete's husband, Fernando, was an agricultural scientist and head of the research station at Chianga just outside Huambo. Chianga was part of the university and a new generation of agricultural economists and botanists was trained here by his team to the highest of standards in the years since independence. The campus was set in a park of huge and ancient flowering trees, with laboratories, libraries of rare books and a collection of soil samples in hundreds of glass jars which mapped the different fertility across Angola's contrasting land from northern forest to southern savannah. The night before I was to visit Chianga, Unita placed a mine on the approach road, blowing up the first car to arrive at the research station in the morning. That same night, on the other side of Huambo, they also blew up the International Red Cross office and the clinic at Bomba Alta which made artificial limbs for mine victims. The freshly blackened walls and charred remnants of artificial limbs, like the new gaping hole in the Chianga road, seemed suddenly to bring this war of random killing and destruction even closer than the tens of thousands of maimed and displaced peasants who so visibly peopled Huambo.

The Marcelinos, and their great friend Dr David Bernardino who I was to meet with them, were quite different from anyone I had met in Luanda, either the formal Party contacts through OMA or the cosmopolitan circle of my friend's friends. These people looked and behaved as though from another world – utterly dedicated to the ideals of the MPLA which they had carried since before independence, and so schooled in the acceptance of danger, hardship and sorrow that they were unmentioned. No civilians lived a life closer to the dangers and privations of the front line, but they had chosen that life in Huambo, in part in solidarity with the peasants who could not choose where they lived. Dr Bernardino was a socialist, a painter, a writer, a lover of music and ballet, as his small house in the centre of town immediately revealed when we went there that evening. On big panels on one wall he had painted Picasso-like dancing people with trumpets and horns against a background of blue lakes and black mountains, while on another was a solitary, reflective zebra. His chosen work was in a small primary healthcare clinic which he had built on the edge of Huambo town where the road disappeared into high grass and a red earth track winds past mud and wattle huts, patches of maize and the waving fronds of banana trees. Every day he was here, treating malaria and malnutrition, the diseases of the poor and, under the wattle roof built to shade the adjoining courtyard, overseeing the huge pots of food for the dozens of skinny children who came in every day. But at the same time he was one of Huambo's links to the outside world where his specialised research on goitre was internationally known.

Ten years later, these three, whose fierce idealism had made them the soul of Huambo, were assassinated by Unita in two separate attacks. The killers got away with impunity. The quietly heroic lives of Dr Bernardino and the Marcelinos, and the manner of their deaths, symbolise the chance that Angola had and lost, to become a leader of a post-colonial Africa which put its millions of poor and deprived at the top of the continental agenda. That hope was brutally undermined in those years when South African-led destabilisation by Unita flourished and matured into a force which broke the state of Angola. These killings symbolised Unita's determination to have Angola on their own terms. Racism, culture, ideology all played a part in these assassinations. For David and the Marcelinos their work, which gave their lives meaning, their pleasures of classical music and movies`like *Babette's Feast*, their libraries, their internationalism, their uncompromising honesty, gave them an unbreakable independence from any central power. The organisations they ran – Chianga, OMA, the clinic – were all ones which promised ordinary people, if not a taste of that independence, at least the chance of making choices and a better future for themselves. But the idea of choices and personal autonomy for Angola's peasants ran smack up against Unita's totalitarian concepts and practices – Huambo was marked for a disastrous clash. But in 1984 no one seemed to foresee that the disaster could get worse. Everyone lived in the present, and it was made bearable by the thought that the war would be over just as soon as South Africa achieved majority rule.

The following week I flew north in a small plane, invited by the MPLA's Organising Secretary, Lucio Lara, who had had a letter introducing me from his old friend from the guerrilla struggle, the British historian Basil Davidson, and who was visiting peasant cooperatives organised by the Party. Lara, tall, spare, aesthetic, with a heavy Latin moustache, was the man who epitomised the heroic Angola which lived so long in the imagination of so many Africans across the continent. He was the leading ideologue in the MPLA from the years of the guerrilla struggle in the forests of Cabinda and the bush of eastern Angola, and the man best known and trusted by the top Cuban leadership, many of whom were part of Angola's fight for independence from those days. 'L'Afrique profonde, that's what they always wanted Angola to be,' he once said to me, much later, encapsulating decades of what he had fought against. 'L'Afrique profonde' sums up every stereotype of black Africa, from Conrad's *Heart of Darkness* through Idi Amin's evil buffoonery, Bokassa and cannibalism, the savagery of Doe's beach executions of his predecessors and his own gruesome end captured on video – crude leadership of ignorant, child-like people. Unita's primitive fascism, in which all potential rivals to Jonas Savimbi were killed and social control maintained by the terror of public burning of women as witches, and kidnapping which wrested young men and girls out of family and community, created totally dependent people, devoid of free will, emotionally annihilated.

The town of Malange was holding the line against L'Afrique profonde in 1984. It was even colder than Huambo and lost in mist and rain. The pot-holed roads, broken buildings and closed shops told the same story of a community under virtual siege. But the scent of despair was not there. This was a town fighting a war well understood as fired by imperialism. On the walls of the main street huge, painted murals of Angola's first President, Agostinho Neto, Fidel Castro, and Che Guevara, shouted defiance at the South Africans, Unita and their US backers. In the main square, flame trees shaded a war memorial made entirely of old AK47 rifles and spent rounds which commemorated the Cuban soldiers who had given their lives here. As in Huambo the defence of the town was assured by a Cuban garrison and there was also a clandestine camp of South African African National Congress guerrillas in the province.

We stayed in the Governor's palace, a chateau crumbling from years with no maintenance but with beautiful, long rooms filled with old, ornate Portuguese sofas, armchairs and cloudy mirrors. Meals were at a long table filled with the Governor's staff and Party officials and the talk, in several languages, was of the difficult and deteriorating economic and security situation in the province, and of the uneasy stand-off in the south of the country where, as Iko Carreira had explained, occupying South African forces had not begun to pull back over the border to Namibia as they had promised in negotiations earlier in the year.

Lucio Lara spent two days driving round cooperative farms with the province Governor and MPLA Party officials, looking at water taps, tractors, ploughs and harrows and listening to peasant leaders talk and talk of their difficulties. Shortages of fuel and spare parts for tractors, kerosene for lamps, soap, salt and other necessities meant that many of the cooperatives were doing poorly. The war was encroaching on their rich agricultural province – roads were no longer safe to travel, young men and boys had been kidnapped by Unita and never seen again, supplies of inputs needed for the farms and which should come from Luanda were scarce. Through hours of sitting in farm courtyards Lara barely spoke, but listened as the complaints came thick and fast with no fear of the man in authority. The peasants were angry and asking for more military action against Unita, against the South Africans, to safeguard their land and crops from further deterioration. Here was another vision of what the Party meant to people, quite different from the formality I had been shown before. Here the MPLA was the centre of people's lives, their security, their entry into a new world of organised farming, and the faith in the leadership was touching and unmistakable. On the last day, as he went into the closing meeting with the Governor and Party, Lara sent me off to see one of Angola's wonders, the Calendula waterfall. We drove along a battered, tarmac road past forests of huge, flowering trees and fields of maize and coffee. When we got out of the car to walk down to Calendula for a moment the realities behind the escort of two dozen soldiers, the strict orders not to step beyond the path because of the danger of mines, and to start back well before dark, were forgotten before the beauty of the huge, thundering falls, iridescent in the sun and framed by giant ferns and flowering pink and white trees. It was a beauty that would be unseen for years a few months later as Unita moved deeper into the province, cutting off Calendula and more roads and farming areas. Beautiful Calendula vanished into L'Afrique profonde.

CHAPTER 1

Birth of Africa's Brightest Hope
1975–76

When the red and black flag with the yellow star representing independent Angola was raised over Luanda on 11 November 1975, ending the repressive blood-soaked years of Portuguese colonialism, it was a victory for an African liberation movement, but a victory with a political and emotional resonance well beyond the continent. Third World countries from Latin America to Asia, struggling with the economic and social tangles they were left in after colonialism, identified with the unequal nature of the Angolan struggle. And Angola's hard-won independence was a pledge to millions further south on the continent that the liberation of the rest of Africa was possible. The illegal white regime of Ian Smith in Rhodesia and the apartheid regime in South Africa, which also occupied Namibia, would, Africans believed, be the next to be swept away by an inexorable historical force. In Angola, as in Vietnam, guerrillas had won a war essentially against the United States and its interests, against all the odds. The victory of the Popular Movement for the Liberation of Angola (MPLA) was part of what engendered the new mood of confidence sweeping the Third World and which led over the next few years to violent uprisings and changes in the balance of power within the societies of Iran, Ethiopia, Ghana, Liberia, Grenada and Nicaragua.

The volunteer army of the MPLA had fought the Portuguese in the deep forests of Cabinda and the vast, empty grasslands of eastern Angola for more than a decade, contributing to the collapse of the Portuguese empire, sent on its way by the coup against the fascist regime in Lisbon in April 1974. The Angolan guerrillas, men and women, black and white, went on to worst the most powerful military force in Africa – that of apartheid South Africa – the well-equipped regular army of Zaire, two rival Angolan forces – those of Unita and the FNLA which had mercenaries, advisers, and equipment provided by the CIA – the French intelligence services and the Chinese government. Only in the chaotic decolonisation of the Belgian Congo in the 1960s had Africa seen such an international struggle for the soul of a country. Like the Congo (which later became Zaire) Angola's great natural resources –

1

including oil and diamonds – its size and its strategic location made it a prize so tempting that the big powers did not for a moment dream of leaving its future direction to Angolans. But unlike the Congo Angola had a powerfully intellectual leader – the poet/doctor/guerrilla fighter Agostinho Neto, whose life's work was to give Angolans their independence and who dared to take the high risk of inviting the Cuban military to Angola to help safeguard it and prevent a breakdown of society as had happened in the Congo before and after the death of Patrice Lumumba. In the eight months running up to independence in November 1975 Angola was on the brink of just such another catastrophe as a transitional power-sharing agreement made between the three Angolan parties at Alvor in January 1975 collapsed.

In their subsequent attempts to justify 20 years of refusing diplomatic links with Angola and 20 years of material and diplomatic aid to those who had destroyed the country, the Americans falsified the history of 1975 to create a Soviet and Cuban threat to the region which, at the height of the Cold War, had to be countered. The MPLA, they charged, never intended to share power with the other two parties and was planning with the Soviets and Cubans to crush the National Liberation Front of Angola (FNLA) and Unita militarily, giving the Soviet Union a strategic foothold in a key region of Africa. The realities were very different. In Washington in January 1975, Henry Kissinger and the Committee of 40 authorised $300,000 for the MPLA's main rival group, the FNLA. The FNLA leader, Holden Roberto, had been on the CIA payroll since 1961 with an annual stipend of $10,000 and was the brother-in-law of another of their clients, President Mobutu of Zaire. The FNLA had its base in Zaire and its military operations, such as they were against the Portuguese, were run from there. The American money and encouragement meant a substantial upgrading of its operations in 1975 against the MPLA, its nominal partner in the transitional government. Simultaneously the Americans also stepped up support for Unita, and throughout the year ambushes and assassinations of the MPLA by its two rivals destabilised the country and made a mockery of power-sharing within the transitional government. And, most importantly, the Americans gave the nod to Pretoria to mount an ambitious military adventure over the Namibian border in support of its two Angolan proxies.

On the MPLA side a handful of Cuban instructors had indeed been with the guerrillas since the early days of the liberation war in Cabinda, but it was the invasion of regular South African troops ten miles inside southern Angola on 5 August 1975, followed by further waves on 14 October and 23 October with armoured vehicles and artillery moving north towards Luanda, which triggered the sending of 480 Cuban instructors who arrived in mid-October in three Cuban ships.

Then, as the threat to the MPLA in the capital intensified (with Zairian units crossing the northern border in a joint operation with the FNLA which brought three columns of armoured cars and artillery sweeping to Caxito, within 30 miles of Luanda), the Cuban Central Committee met on 5 November and decided to dispatch the first Cuban fighting unit to Angola. Six hundred and fifty men left at once in three old four-engine Cubana planes, charged by Fidel Castro with the daunting mission of at all costs stopping the South Africans and Zairians reaching Luanda before 11 November, the day independence from Portugal was to be formally declared. Zaire then had 11,200 troops in Angola and South Africa about 6,000. On the very eve of Independence Day the Zairians, with a 26-man South African logistical support team, launched the decisive battle for control of Luanda, attempting to take Quifangondo, the site of the capital's water supply only 15 miles from Luanda. The Zairian regular army made a simultaneous attack in the oil enclave of Cabinda in support of the secessionist movement FLEC. The South Africans meanwhile fought their way up the coast from the south where they had taken the provincial capitals of Lubango and Namibe, but were halted 150 miles from Luanda by blown-up bridges.

In all three theatres – the north, Cabinda and the south – the Cubans were key to the turning of the military tide which allowed the MPLA to become the legitimate government when independence was declared, because they were in control of Luanda. The Portuguese flag was lowered on the afternoon of 11 November and High Commissioner Admiral Leonel Gomes Cardoso stepped onto a frigate and sailed out of Luanda's semi-circular bay – crowded with cargo ships taking on board Portuguese possessions – back to Europe. Five hundred years of Portuguese rule in Angola was over and at midnight the President of the MPLA, Agostinho Neto, proclaimed the country independent. Shortly afterwards, Lucio Lara, one of the historic leaders of the anti-colonial struggle and Secretary of the MPLA's Political Bureau, in the name of the party's Central Committee invested Neto as President of the People's Republic.

Shadows lay over the exhilaration, as evident as the gunfire audible to the north of the city. Most of the skilled Portuguese and even some of the few skilled Angolans had left in the run-up to independence so that the service sector and agricultural exporting sector of the economy had virtually collapsed. The impoverished urban suburbs and the subsistence farming of the rural areas offered no foundation for a new modern state to be run by inexperienced cadres returning from exile, jail or the bush war. But much worse, 11 November and independence were not seen as definitive turning points by the MPLA's enemies. In the next month one of the ugliest episodes of the war began: one which would end in a Luanda court room on 10 July 1976 with four mercenaries sentenced to execution and nine to prison terms of up to 30 years.

No one could have foreseen that these American and British men were the symbols of what was to come to independent Angola from the outside world. No one could have foreseen that the years of sacrifice and death were only just beginning and that over the next 20 years the sacrifices and deaths would be greater every single year.

Those 13 men in the dock in Luanda in mid-1976 symbolised the end of the war of ideals in which the choices were clear between an independence to be fashioned on Africa's own terms or one which would have put the country, with its fabulous riches of oil, diamonds and minerals, under the wing of apartheid South Africa. But the interests which lay behind these men in 1975 were strong enough to transform that war into another one which held the whole region in thrall for two decades. The new phase was first fired by apartheid South Africa's struggle for regional domination, then by the Cold War, then by the ambition of one man, Jonas Savimbi, and by the international community's extraordinary complicity with his goals. Along the way Angola was destroyed, its independence, socialism, and non-racialism were sacrificed, its sovereignty lost. A wild capitalism was allowed to flourish and ethnic origins became of paramount importance.

In the solemn atmosphere of the court in Luanda two cultures clashed as some of the Western world's most irresponsible psychopaths and rejects of society faced a carefully prepared dossier of their crimes presented with impeccable formality by soldiers and peasants whose lives had been put on the line by these foreigners who could not even have found Angola on a map, much less explained why they were there. For a start the mercenaries were well-treated by their captors, in sharp contrast to the brutalities which they had both experienced and dealt out themselves long before they had even signed up on the other side of this far away war.

A fifty-strong International Commission of Inquiry on Mercenaries was constituted in Luanda in May 1976. Chosen some as individuals, some as representatives of their government, they were eminent judges, lawyers, professors, writers and others from around the world. Like the MPLA they were living a moment of idealism and optimism in which a different world from the one which produced these mercenaries had been born. Their report was intended to influence events in Africa far beyond Angola and to stem, at least briefly, the flood of mercenaries then heading for work in Ian Smith's Rhodesia as it resisted majority rule. The distinguished international profile of the Commission was also a legitimating tool for the actual trial of the mercenaries by the new system of justice in the brand new state. The People's Revolutionary Tribunal had six judges. The Presiding Judge, Texeiro da Silva, was Angola's Attorney General, a quiet, courteous man who never raised his voice or showed a flicker of irritation at the defendants or their lawyers. The others were two soldiers, a member of the Angolan Women's Organisation (OMA) and two administrators. Three of the six had legal training. The Public Prosecutor was one of the MPLA's intellectual stars, the brilliant, flamboyant writer Manuel Rui Alves Monteiro, once Minister of Information and then head of the Department of External Affairs. At one point he asked the mercenaries about their ideological beliefs, but was met only with blank, uncomprehending stares. No such concept was part of the mental world of these limited men. All of them were in Angola primarily for the money: £200 a week for officers, £150 for privates and a promised bonus of £25,000 for any man who captured a Russian. They were recruited mainly through newspaper advertisements by middlemen well enough connected to the British authorities to be able to take through immigration and customs men who had no passports and others who were actually wanted by the police. In the second group of 20 men, 11 were either without passports or wanted. The middlemen were themselves paid £200–300 per man recruited through International Security Organisation headed by John Banks, the key man in sending British cannon fodder to Holden Roberto and his FNLA. Everyone was paid in new dollar notes through the US embassy in Kinshasa. Most of the mercenaries were former soldiers, two were MI6 agents (one of whom was killed and the other wounded), others had no experience of war and simply went to pieces in the chaos and brutality of the Angola/Zaire border. Fourteen paid with their lives on the orders of the most notorious of the psychopaths, a former private in the British army, Costas Georgiou, who arrived in Zaire with four others in December, a month after Angolan independence. He began to call himself 'Colonel Callan' and was introduced by Holden Roberto to the mercenaries who came later in John Banks' groups, or in the small group from the US, as his Commandant. Just how desperate the situation of the FNLA then was could be seen not only in Callan's appointment but also in his later admission under questioning that the FNLA had only about 100 men under arms at that point. In addition there were Portuguese fascist mercenaries of the Portuguese Liberation Army (ELN) with the FLNA. Between 16 January and 10 February another 185 mercenaries arrived, despite the now open disapproval by some in the US of the CIA policy which lay behind the recruitment of mercenaries for Angola, and the passing of the Clark Amendment on 9 February 1976 which specifically outlawed such US arming of opposition groups. However, according to John Stockwell (the CIA's main man on the spot), on 11 February the CIA promised Savimbi another million dollars in arms and money and on 18 February Henry Kissinger ordered the CIA in Kinshasa to assure Savimbi that he would continue to get US support as long as Unita could keep up effective resistance to the MPLA.

The chaotic collapse of the military option by the two rival parties to the MPLA was thus not enough to deter their backers or their own leaders. In the Alice-in-Wonderland scene of Angola in late 1975, Unita/FNLA had declared independence in Huambo on November 11 and in many places in the south a Unita flag was raised though no civilian administration was even attempted. Their Government of the Democratic People's Republic of Angola was a creation of the CIA, urged on two reluctant parties whose relations with each other were poor and, recognised by not one country. Within a month the two allies were fighting each other. War spread across the Central Highlands as the MPLA and the Cubans moved to consolidate independence. The South African columns fought on for another month before the turning of the tide of US policy became inescapable, with a Senate vote on 19 December cutting off aid to Angolan opposition groups, and before Nigeria, briefly led by the left-leaning soldier Murtala Mohamed, recognised the MPLA government on 27 November and swung the mood in Africa. The South African link had been fatal to the image of Unita and FNLA. An OAU special summit on Angola the following month saw the collapse of the proposal put forward by Savimbi's friends in the leadership of Zambia and Côte D'Ivoire for a coalition government, despite much lobbying behind the scenes of the conference by the CIA, still determined that the MPLA should not enjoy power alone. At the end of December the South African military commander finally told Savimbi that he was going to pull his units out of their forward position at Cala, 130 miles north of Huambo. By the end of January the South Africans were on the move southwards and by the end of March they were all out. Twenty-nine of them had been killed in action and 14 in accidents since the previous July.

The other outside backers were slower to give up. Not only were the fated FNLA mercenaries still arriving in the north from Britain and the US, but France sent four missile-firing helicopters to Kinshasa for Unita as late as January 1976. However, the Israeli pilots who had been promised to fly them never materialised, nor did the American C130 transport plane and heavy artillery and Redeye missiles promised by the Americans. Western policy was in utter confusion. The CIA's John Stockwell was open in his scorn for all the agency's clients. Nonetheless, stockpiled supplies for the anti-MPLA war were still flown in to Unita from Kinshasa over the next month and 20 French mercenaries were brought in for rapid training of Unita personnel on the new equipment. They left in short order, quickly evaluating the chance of survival being very low, and advised Savimbi to fly out with them and bide his time in exile. He refused.

It took until 8 February 1976 for the MPLA and Cuban troops, supported by helicopters and MIG fighter planes, to take control of Huambo. Savimbi led his Unita troops in a retreat to the nearby town of Vila Nova. Two days later he announced the beginning of a new war which would be fought from the bush. The MPLA soldiers arriving in Huambo found mass graves, banks and stores looted and a litany of stories of MPLA officials, especially Umbundus, who had been targeted by Unita or FNLA. It was the same story as the MPLA took control of other important towns such as Benguela and Lobito on the coast. In the port of Lobito, Unita was accused of at least 500 summary executions of people believed to be MPLA sympathisers in the last weeks before Unita was forced to flee. After a few weeks regrouping in the town of Gago Coutinho the remnants of Savimbi's army and their families were bombed in the town as they defiantly celebrated the symbolic date of 13 March, when the movement was founded. It was time to move on and to hide.

From the deep bush Savimbi produced a defiant manifesto which threatened 'there will be no peace in Angola, no economic development, no railroad traffic, no working harbours, while the Luanda regime hangs on to power thanks to Cuban soldiers and Russian armour and fighter planes'. At the time they were the empty words of a desperate man with no fighting capacity and no allies. By mid-April even Zambia, long a haven for Unita refugees, had recognised the MPLA government. And, with the South Africans finally out, the Cubans and Angolans agreed on a programmed reduction of Cuban forces to bring them down by a third within a year.

Meanwhile in Luanda thousands of Cuban civilians joined the MPLA's returning exiles and guerrilla fighters in the very different battle to rebuild a society on the ruins of what the Portuguese had left behind. Blocks of flats were built at record speed by Cubans, bridges were rebuilt in many provinces and teachers and doctors began to fan out across the country. Other Cubans worked in every Ministry. Volunteers were young enthusiasts, women as often as men, and in many cases had left a child at home with a grandmother for their two years in Angola. Young women with pink earrings and ponytails, young men almost fresh out of university, they were awed by the scale of the problems they confronted, but buoyed up by a sense of mission. 'Internationalism' was a vocation of which they were intensely proud. Their jobs were kept for their return and while they were away their normal government salary was paid into their account in Havana, plus 20 per cent extra for overtime. They certainly earned it. One after another the doctors, in particular, told of seven-day working weeks, including several nights a week spent at their hospitals. In Angola they received an allowance in local currency which easily covered their needs and every year they had a month's holiday in Cuba. They faced the extremely difficult working conditions with a matter-of-fact shrug and quickly made themselves indispensable and much loved. In the intensity of those heady days many were ready to volunteer for another tour long before the first had finished. 'It will be very hard to leave Angola, you make very deep friendships in this kind of work,' said one young woman, mother of a six-year-old back in Havana who she talked about with pleasure but no anxiety. 'You don't need to worry about them, they are very well supported. There is a provincial structure which visits all the children of international-ists, plus our employer, the Ministry of Health, also has an obligation to look after our child – it is double security beyond the family.'

Exhilaration for Angolans was mixed with moments of doubt, faced with the sheer size of Luanda, its tree-lined streets sweeping down to the bay, its office blocks, shops and banks closed, the complex world of a capital city stripped of so much of its infrastructure by bitter departing colonisers. But the doubts were pushed aside by the excitement of the new world they were confident they could make and the sweetness of reunions of families and friends parted for years. Tens of thousands of people had come out of Portuguese prisons, some from as far away as the Cape Verde islands, and exiles returned from many African countries. Luanda was a bustling, busy city, soon filled with East European trucks and buses vying for space with battered cars and noisy motorbikes. The pavements were full too, with women in bright cloth wrapped around as a skirt, soldiers and innumerable children. On the walls great murals were painted telling the story of the war or depicting Agostinho Neto, Fidel Castro or Che Guevara and giant slogans hailed 'People's Power' and 'International Solidarity with the Revolution'. The atmosphere of new confidence was palpable. 'Camarade' was the greeting for everyone – one word cutting through the hierarchies which had been a hallmark of Portuguese colonialism.

A wave of new exiles arrived too, in particular South Africans from the African National Congress (ANC) for whom, like the Swapo guerrillas of Namibia, Angola was to become a home from home and their most important military training base for a decade. They adopted this new world with gusto. For the young men and women coming out of apartheid's townships it was a world of equality and easy informality beyond their dreams. The VIP lounge of Luanda airport was often like an ANC reception room, with Oliver

Tambo, Joe Slovo, Joe Modise or Ronnie Kasrils half-hidden in the great brown leather sofas and using the last minutes before the arrival or departure of a flight to their headquarters in Lusaka for hurried consultations with the men in charge of their camps in remote parts of Angola. The camps were run by the ANC with some Cuban contingents attached as military trainers. They were spartan places where education and discipline were the prime goals. Military techniques were only part of a more general political training. There was little contact with local Angolans as the camps were self-sufficient, with tinned food from the Soviet Union and China brought from Luanda, baboons and python killed for meat and grain and vegetables grown in camp.

For the South Africans, focused primarily on when they would be able to return and fight inside their own country, there was a constant reminder of how high the stakes were in what had become a regional war as South Africa kept up a low-level aggression inside Angola. In the three years after their columns withdrew from Angola in March 1976 there were 193 armed mine-laying operations, 21 border crossings from Namibia, seven bombing raids, and one large-scale operation of both ground and air units. Hundreds of Angolans and hundreds more refugees from Rhodesia and Namibia were killed in this period of undeclared war.

The unfolding regional war of the late 1970s was South Africa's unfinished business of its attempt to take over in Angola in 1975, but it also took on the deteriorating security situation at home as resistance to apartheid grew more defiant within the townships and the ANC's external leadership began to pose a challenge which could not be ignored. But it was the flowering of the Cold War, and in particular the election of Ronald Reagan as US President in 1980, which opened the next scene of Angola's deepening tragedy.

CHAPTER 2

The Remaking of Unita 1976–85

Just a year after the ignominious South African retreat from Angola, Savimbi, fresh from his long march through the bush to save the remnants of his Unita movement, was staying at the Grosvenor House Hotel in London with one of the key background players in the Angolan war, a discreet Côte D'Ivoire official. Savimbi gave a briefing to his astonished representative in London, Antonio da Costa Fernandes, that new support was coming to Unita from Pretoria to restart the war. Costa Fernandes was one of the closest of Savimbi's associates and his surprise at the decision to risk Unita's credibility in Africa by again entering an alliance with the apartheid regime illustrates the extent to which Savimbi was a lone operator with little or no taste for consultation on Unita's future. Costa Fernandes had been with Savimbi in Switzerland as a student and in November 1963 the two men had gone on a weekend retreat in the mountains together to plan their opposition to Portuguese colonialism. Together over that weekend they wrote the statutes on which Unita was based and which they believed would form a movement more popular and less intellectual than the MPLA. They were heavily influenced at the time by Mao, and among the provisions from those days, which seemed increasingly remote in London in 1977, were two which said that the leadership must all have military training and must operate within the country. Costa Fernandes had been the man who recruited in the refugee camps of Zambia for the first group of Unita men to go to China for military training and was among the 15 who went.

At the same time in 1977, Jeremias Chitunda, who was Unita's representative in America both for the UN and the US, succeeded in convincing Washington to shift its support definitively from the FNLA, badly discredited by the mercenaries' affair, to Unita. For both Pretoria and Washington, still smarting from the debacle of the disastrous military campaign of 1975–76, the new gamble was made largely on the personality of Savimbi. His personal bravery, his ruthlessness, his vaulting ambition and his mastery of public relations for an international audience had been demonstrated in the five months of his long march with the remnants of his troops after they were bombed by the MPLA in March 1976. Before starting the march he had announced the executions, by an all-woman firing squad, of 17 captured Cuban soldiers. It was a communiqué intended to catch attention, to shock, and to establish Savimbi's credentials as a bulwark against the Cuban presence in Angola. The one-time Maoist had thus publicly marked himself out for the Americans as one of the most significant anti-communists in Africa. Then, having refused to go into exile himself, with the last French mercenaries he had, by willpower and coercion, kept alive and moving several thousand weakened and dispirited followers in an almost empty area of Angola. There were uncounted deaths and the Unita cause had never been at a lower ebb, but Savimbi was only biding his time for foreign backers to return to him. The South Africans, as he explained in London, were the convenient stop-gaps whose military support would allow Unita to become a factor to conjure with again in the Angolan situation.

It was thanks to the Cold War that Western money subsequently began to flow in to the virtually non-existent Unita army. With the help of the French secret service and a collection of US Arab clients, a small river of cash bought quantities of grenades, rockets, mortars and sophisticated weapons, including anti-tank missiles. Tens of thousands of youths were systematically kidnapped from towns and villages to form the new Unita army in the empty lands of the south, and thousands of young girls taken with them were to form the basis of sexual and family life in an almost unpopulated place. This vast movement of population was a phenomenon unseen and unheard of by outsiders, and even in Angola itself the weak new state often did not know much of what happened in remote areas. Isolated reports of kidnappings made little impact at home or abroad. The serious weakness of the MPLA in communicating with the rest of the world began to emerge as a key factor in the distortion of Angola's realities, and one which would dog the regime for 20 years and hand the propaganda specialists of the CIA and Pretoria a blank sheet on which to write their version of Angola's story.

By March 1979 the South Africans were ready to create Jamba, the Potemkin village in the southeast corner of Angola which was to be Savimbi's headquarters for 13 years. It was a desolate place with no agricultural base and no convenient water supply, chosen entirely for its geographical location – as far from Luanda as possible and within easy reach of the South African bases in occupied Namibia and the Caprivi Strip. Protected from the Angolan military by South African air cover flying from northern Namibia, Jamba became the public relations face of Unita shown to journalists and Western backers of all sorts flown in for a day or two and impressed by a well-supplied bush hospital, schools, a stadium, traffic lights and an airport with Unita immigration facilities. But the centrepiece of the Jamba experience was Savimbi himself. He honed his public relations skills in press conferences and interviews, mainly with the lazy and compliant Johannesburg press corps or selected European and American journalists keen on the anti-communist cause of the time. His fluent duplicity was swallowed uncritically by many journalists who should have known better than to help build his reputation as the committed democrat and soldier/intellectual fighting for an Angola free of Soviet and Cuban domination. In fact Savimbi's image and the entire creation of Jamba was South Africa's, and on a day to day basis it depended entirely upon Pretoria and the CIA.

The other side of Jamba, which the outsiders on the day trips did not see or hear about, was its role as the centre of a highly organised and repressive terror machine which spared not even the families of the leadership from sudden disappearances, interrogations, months in underground pit prisons and numerous deaths, some in public ceremonies designed to cement the organisation on the basis of fear. Accusations of witchcraft were commonly brought against women and even children who were then brought to Jamba's stadium, doused in petrol beside piles of firewood and set alight. Savimbi was himself presiding over these medieval killing ceremonies, suddenly a different man from the charismatic multi-lingual charmer of foreign journalists, right-wing American Congressmen and the South African leaders who were making him into a key player in their strategy to defeat radical nationalism both at home and across the region.

Besides their training of Unita's raw youths, the South African military began a series of invasions and sabotage of Angola by their own forces: in May 1978 they attacked a Swapo refugee camp at Cassinga with two C130 transport planes, 14 helicopters, 9 Mirage fighter planes and 200 paratroopers, killing 612 Namibian refugees, 12 Angolan soldiers and 3 civilians, and wounding another 700 people in a six-hour killing spree; the following year in a Zimbabwean refugee camp at Boma in the east 198 refugees were killed and 600 wounded in a joint Rhodesian/South African bombing raid; in 1979 the southern towns of Lubango and Xangongo were bombed; Operation Smokeshell was launched in 1980, targeting villages, shops and schools in Cunene province; Operation Protea in August 1981 was the creation of a buffer zone south of the Cunene river with an invasion of 11,000 men with tanks and troop carriers; Luanda's oil refinery was sabotaged in the same year; Operation Smokescreen penetrated deep inside the country in 1982; the Lomaum dam was blown up in 1983; Operation Askari was another invasion the same year. Bombing raids and mine-laying operations took place regularly, causing hundreds of mainly civilian casualties. The southern strip of the country, the agricultural provinces of

Cuando Cubango, Cunene, Namibe and Huila, near the Namibian border, were thus intermittently occupied by Pretoria's troops. Much of the population fled from the worst affected areas into makeshift camps for displaced people.

The war which touched most Angolans in the late 1970s and early 1980s, however, was a different phenomenon from either the guerrilla war against the Portuguese, or the intense fighting of the period around independence with the tanks and heavy artillery brought into the country by the South African and Zairian armies which fought pitched battles with the MPLA and the Cubans, or the new South African attacks. In Washington and in Europe people began to talk and write about Low Intensity Conflict – the new fashion in Western interference in Third World countries, one which kept costs minimal for the sponsor of the war and promised the fatal undermining of the government by proxy forces. Angola was a perfect theatre for LIC – like Mozambique and Nicaragua, a country remote enough to ensure that little about its consequences would filter back to Western public opinion. Unita terror tactics in rural areas began the systematic destruction of the lives of peasant families, people who knew nothing of the international political context of the Cold War in which they were expendable.

Rosa was a smiling seven-year-old, living in a village in the Central Highlands. Great primal forests of flowering trees and pink/grey grasslands taller than a child, stretching to the horizon through the clear, high altitude air, spoke of a world of ancient harmonies, now combined with the aspirations of education and change promised with independence by the MPLA. But Rosa's world fell apart the day Unita attacked her village. Rosa's mother, seeing armed men coming towards the cluster of huts, from where she was working in the fields, ran with her daughter to warn her friends. But she was caught by the soldiers and Rosa watched them cut off her mother's hand, then her ear, then her breast, then her arm and leg. Years later, living in an orphanage in Bié, Rosa was restless, still sleeping badly, had sudden screaming fits and could not go to school because she could not concentrate or take anything in. The sight of a military uniform or a white face made her scream and run out of the room. Her future was utterly bleak and the women who worked in the orphanage mourned their inability to penetrate her madness.

Natalia was seven or eight the night Unita came to her house, also in the Central Highlands, and similarly destroyed her world and expectations. She lived in a little hamlet and her family had a small-holding growing maize, cassava and vegetables. One night a group of Unita soldiers burst into the hut where she was with her three smallest brothers. 'Where are your father and mother?,' the men asked. Natalia replied, 'My mother is dead and my father is not here.' But the soldiers pushed past her into an inner room where they found her parents. Both of them were shot dead in front of the children. The soldiers then left, taking what food there was as well as various other things from the hut. Natalia's family, wiped out in a few moments just for a little food, had been Unita supporters like everyone around them in Bailundo, and even had two older boys already serving in the Unita army. The random attack made no sense to the victims, but served to terrorise a whole community and to establish Unita as a force to be feared. Natalia and her brothers were initially taken in by an aunt, but she could not manage the four orphans as well as her own children and gave Natalia away as a small servant to a woman who lived in Luanda. Separated from her brothers and far from home, Natalia grew too sad even to be useful as a kitchen maid, and finally ended up in an orphanage. Four or five years after her parents' death she was still saying she thought about her mother every single day and every night before falling asleep.

The liberation war against the Portuguese had barely touched Bié, though in the aftermath of Unita's brief seizure of Huambo at independence in November 1975 and their flight south three months later, the splitting of families and scattering of children, which was to give Angola a huge orphanage population over the next 20 years, began even here. In 1976, Carlinda, a psychiatric social worker, was living in Bié. 'It was dusk when the military truck drew up outside our orphanage and a group of government soldiers walked in carrying some children they had found left in a village after a fire fight with Unita. Those soldiers were so sweet with them, so concerned that they should be in a safe place, so unconscious of whether they were Unita children, I have never forgotten that touching scene. Those soldiers had had very good childhoods of their own,' she recounted 20 years later with nostalgia for an era of safety and community responsibility lost almost without trace.

But less than a decade after independence this remote province of rich farm lands was paying a heavy price for its position on the route used by Unita between its southern stronghold of Jamba, maintained by the South Africans, and pockets of territory in the northeast by the Zaire border, maintained with CIA supplies. The orphanages in Bié and Huambo provinces told the story of what happened along Unita's route in the mid-1980s. Gigi was responsible for orphaned and abandoned children in Bié province and the orphanages in the towns of Cuito, Kamakupa and Katabola. She described how Unita attacked these towns over and over again and invariably targeted the orphanages, knowing that there would always be food in them because they were a priority for the government social services department. During one attack the director of an orphanage was beaten up and Unita then stripped the orphanage of everything and kidnapped seven children, the cook and two of the nursery staff. In another attack children were questioned about the name of the director of their orphanage, when she visited and what sort of car she had. Clearly an ambush was planned. Once, hearing gunfire, children and staff ran to hide by the river, but six children fell in and were drowned. Four more children were lost in the confusion and the orphanage staff assumed they must have been taken by Unita. In the course of one flight a young boy, Ricardo, stepped on a mine and lost a leg. He also lost a sister that same day – she was among those who disappeared. Seven children from that one orphanage lost legs in mine accidents. They all survived, but their chances of getting an artificial limb and the possibility of a relatively normal life were extremely slim. (Even in the most deprived of circumstances, though, some children managed extraordinary feats of personal fulfilment. Ricardo, for instance, studied hard and passed the sixth class.) Another of Gigi's orphanages, Katabola, was attacked one night, with a grenade thrown in the main door and armed men standing at the back door. The sole member of staff hid the children in a large bathroom and the lavatories and showers. It was completely dark, but no child cried or spoke, and they were all saved. But daylight showed that everything in the building had been taken, including the babies' milk. After that the government decided that the orphanages in the countryside were to be closed and all the children were taken to the orphanage in the provincial capital.

Many of the children in Angola's orphanages are survivors of Unita kidnappings, children who have lived through separations and traumas which have turned them into premature adults struggling to get control of their lives. Joao, aged eleven, for instance, described being seized with five other boys outside his home in Malange by a group of Unita soldiers. 'My mother began to cry, but there was nothing they could do – they said they would kill me if my parents tried to get help. We were tied together with a rope around our waists. They took some other children, including girls, and we walked for five days until we came to a base.' Joao was told that he had now left his mother and his father and would go to Jamba to study. There were other kidnapped children in the base and the older ones were given military training. But Joao was told to work so that he would be given food. He chopped wood, carried water and swept. He was given only maize porridge to eat and said he was very hungry. He finally ran away alone and after two days walking found a *soba* (traditional elder) and asked him what to do. He was taken to a government military camp and finally to an orphanage in Luanda.

Joao's friend in the orphanage, Mendonca, also eleven, had a similar story of being kidnapped while playing football with some friends. Seven boys were kidnapped with him and some cattle driven out of their village. Mendonca walked for several days and was taken to several different Unita bases. Finally he was given as 'a son' to a headman and did the same chopping of wood, carrying water and sweeping as Joao. The girls, he said, were given to Unita men as wives. Mendonca did not know how long he spent at the base, but one day while he was there a young man who had tried to escape was caught. As an example he was tied to a tree with his hands behind his back in front of everyone at the base and left there for a long time. After he was released he was ordered to be sent to Jamba. Mendonca nonetheless took the risk of escaping with another child and an older person, and reached a small town where the authorities sent him to the military and then to Luanda.

Compared to many children, these were the lucky survivors, but still their personal history was lost, along with their families and their sense of place.

Hundreds of miles south of Bié, and two hours' drive outside the southern town of Lubango, Lufinda was a cluster of round huts made of bark and wood circling a church used by Catholics, Protestants and Adventists alike. In the early 1980s it became a refuge for many of the 40,000 displaced of Huila province where the South Africans were planning their buffer zone north of the Namibian border to the 13th Parallel running through Lubango, the main air base of southern Angola.

Under the shade of the simple school structure of wattle and branches, the first peasant to tell his story was Juan Jivenga. One night a group of men speaking his own language, Ovimbundo, burst into his hut where two men, two women, and his two nephews, aged 22 and 30, were sleeping. The two nephews were taken away at gun point and have never been seen again. Jivenga, who had been a rich farmer with six cows, two calves and four cattle for ploughing, said the Unita band also took all his livestock, clothes and stores, and set fire to his hut.

Maria Luhuma, a young woman cradling a baby, told the story of how she lost her brother and brother-in-law in Unita attacks on her village. 'They were working in the fields and Unita came and cut my brother with his own machete. They came back to our village many times, usually by night, usually in uniform. Sometimes the group was small and sometimes large. But it was always the same story, killing cows, burning houses, blowing up the school.'

It was indeed the same story – whether in a dozen slow interviews in this one community, or others in camps for displaced people or the swelling squatter slums around Luanda, hospitals, or orphanages – around the country in the early 1980s. It added up to a picture of hundreds, thousands, tens of thousands of unknown histories marked by discontinuities, by upheavals from family and from place, by incomprehension of why horror had come to destroy their lives and their hopes.

Others had their lives broken in a different way, using emotional and sexual weapons. One young married woman was kidnapped with her husband and, because she was beautiful, suffered his murder by a Unita leader who then took her as his wife. She had two children in Jamba whose father was her husband's murderer. It was years before her family in Luanda even knew that she was alive, and then their fear of the possible fate of her children meant that they never allowed any publicity about her captivity. Another young woman was ambushed on the road by Unita and saw her father and two young children murdered. She had left an older child with his grandparents and her husband was studying abroad. She was taken to Jamba and became a nurse, lived with a doctor and had a new family. Her old family presumed she was dead and her husband married again. Years later she escaped from Jamba and came to Luanda with her new family. The confusion of competing ties has left young women like these, and their whole families, torn by emotional conflicts which can never be resolved.

But there was another kind of victim of Unita's ruthless brutality. Well before independence and the new involvement with the South Africans, these victims had slowly understood the danger which faced any possible rival of Jonas Savimbi. Unita's first Chief of Staff was 'Kafundanga' Chingunji, son of one of the most prestigious families in the Central Highlands. His death on the Zambian border in January 1974 was reportedly from cerebral malaria, but his widow and others who saw his swollen, strangely discoloured body, believed he died from poison. Within months the Unita grapevine had named the person who carried out the murder, and the story that it had been done on Savimbi's orders was current. It was typical of the authoritarian atmosphere which surrounded the leader that Kafundanga's widow felt she had no choice but to return to Angola with Savimbi in late 1974, accept the honoured status of widow of the late Chief of Staff, and work in Huambo as one of the leaders of Unita's women's organisation. Savimbi promised her an enquiry into her husband's death at a later stage, when the power struggle with the MPLA was over. It was not the time for her to be thinking about something as momentous as the murder of the organisation's top military man possibly on the orders of his own leader, but the atmosphere of fear and rumour anyway choked off all questions.

Kafundanga's was, however, a death which should have been foretold. His father was one of the few Angolans in the 1950s to go to Portugal for education. He knew Latin, English and French as well as Portuguese, ran his own secondary school, and wanted all his sons to go abroad to study, if possible to the United States or Canada. An educated and confident preacher, and head of Bié province's royal family, Chingunji became a key figure in the growing nationalist movement. He helped people from all three movements working against the Portuguese – MPLA, Unita, and FNLA – and for his pains was imprisoned in Cape Verde by the Portuguese. When he returned from prison to Angola and the Unita-controlled areas of the Central Highlands and the east in the run-up to independence, he still considered Savimbi as a son and refused to listen to the rumours about the Unita leader's possible responsibility for his own son's death.

Chingunji had already lost one son to the independence movement. In 1970, David, known as 'Samwimbila', was killed in what was said to have been an ambush of Portuguese troops devised by Savimbi. David was a top Unita commander, one of the handful trained in China, and had a reputation for being careful and skilful. The Chinese had been open in their appreciation of their trainee and publicly earmarked him as a potential leader of the movement. It was dangerous praise. Numerous soldiers told the family later they had heard him oppose the ambush plan, only to be overruled by Savimbi. Others, who saw the action, later claimed that there was no exchange of fire with the Portuguese, but that David had been the real target of the ambush and had been shot in the back. When he heard the story from some of the soldiers who had been present, Kafundanga confronted Savimbi with the charge that he had ordered his brother's murder. It was a rare confrontation for the Unita leader from someone who considered himself his equal. Savimbi denied it, but Kafundanga was then himself a marked man. Just a year or so later his friend, Caesar Martins, was the next to disappear. Martins was a well-educated Kimbundo from the north, recruited by Kafundanga who was concerned to broaden Unita's base beyond the Central Highlands and the Ovimbundo people. Savimbi declared Martins an American spy. He was killed. As with his brother David's death, it was not long before those involved in the death of Martins came to tell the Chief of Staff who had given them orders.

A third Chingunji brother, Estevao, was called back from his studies in the US at the moment of independence and within two years was also dead, shot in a mysterious ambush. A fourth, Paulo, died in a suspicious car accident in 1975. Another, Tito, was sent abroad as Unita's representative in West Africa, Morocco, France, London and finally the United States. Meanwhile, the old man had fled to Unita's Jamba headquarters after the MPLA consolidated its grip on the Central Highlands in the late 1970s. With his second wife, stepmother to the first four and mother to Tito, he was accused of witchcraft, beaten, run over and killed. The one remaining brother, Dinho, then just 21, vowed vengeance against Savimbi. He paid a very heavy price. He was tortured, had his back broken, and was left in the bush for dead near the eastern town of Licua. However, he survived for several more years and finally was able to tell the story of the decimation of the Chingunji family to his nephew and namesake, Kafundanga's son, who had been brought up in the safety of Zambia.

Rare were the survivors of a challenge of any sort to Savimbi. Among those who disappeared overnight from the top of the leadership in this period were Foreign Minister Jorge Sangumba and another chief of staff, Valdemar Chidondo. More were to come later. One of those who did survive was Savimbi's old friend Fernandes who, after years as the closest of confidants, was suddenly recalled for Unita's 13 March celebrations of the founding of the organisation and found himself imprisoned in one of Jamba's notorious underground pits for 36 days. He was accused of having taken for himself in London money given to Unita – a charge he was later cleared of. But the real reason was more likely to have a been a belated bout of revenge for a confrontation the two men had had shortly before independence. It was over the letters published in the French magazine *Afrique/Asie* which revealed Savimbi's cooperation with the Portuguese military against the MPLA in Operation Timber. Fernandes had been concerned enough at the blow the story dealt to Savimbi's and Unita's credibility, to travel from Zambia, where he was the Unita representative, to the Angolan interior to ask Savimbi for an explanation. Savimbi branded the letters a forgery and managed to convince his friend that the accusations were false. But the confrontation was never forgotten by either man and Fernandes was pulled out of the diplomatic circuit and sent to the front for four years.

By the early 1980s Savimbi was riding high. His gamble with South African support had come off. Unita had come back from the brink of collapse and was for the first time a military force able to destabilise Angola, while Savimbi himself was ready for a key role in a political project considerably bigger than Angola's future: the remaking of the whole Southern African region by the Americans to fit a Cold War vision of its future.

CHAPTER 3

A War of Ideology 1985-87

One night in late May 1985, a 26-year-old South African Special Forces captain, Winan Petrus Johannes Du Toit, one of 14 commandos and a doctor, launched into a small rubber dinghy from a South African Defence Force (SADF) destroyer off the coast of Angola's Cabinda province. From 15 miles off the bay of Malembo, three boats headed for the coast and docked just north of the petrol installations of the US Gulf Oil company, source of 65 per cent of Angola's wealth. This was Operation Argon, prepared since January 1985 with training of the elite team under the young bearded Afrikaner captain in the wild breakers of the remote Saldanha Bay in the Western Cape on South Africa's Atlantic coast.

Five commandos and the doctor took the small boats back to the mother ship that night and the vessel set off to spend the day over the horizon 100 miles off the coast. The other nine men were due to meet them again when they came inland 24 hours later, though, in the event of those on shore not being at the rendezvous, the boats were to return again for them for three nights before giving up, disembarking a cache of food at an emergency point previously agreed and heading back to South Africa in the Israeli-designed destroyer.

Du Toit and his men set off in the dark and in single file through the bush, looking for a hiding place where they could rest until after dark the following day. They were carrying enough explosives to blow the whole Gulf Oil complex to the skies. Their plan was to place two mines at each of the six storage tanks and others on the water pipes for the fire extinguishers, before heading back to the boats under cover of darkness.

The aim of the operation went well beyond the serious material damage it aimed to cause to the Angolan economy, or its effect on undermining the on-going negotiations on the renewal of the contract between Gulf and the Angolan government. If the operation had succeeded, the costs for repairs alone would have been around $200 million, plus $30 million for the oil stocks and about $250 million in lost production while the repairs were carried out. But its greater importance would have been as one of the most ambitious propaganda exercises for Unita which the South Africans had ever mounted. In fact it was to be the only one of the South African sabotage and terrorist operations claimed by Unita as its work, where the full details were ever to be revealed by one of the participants. Only days before Du Toit and his men set out, the Unita representative in Europe announced in Paris that Unita was going to extend its military activities to the oil regions of Soyo and Cabinda. The scene was thus carefully prepared for what would have appeared to be a significant enhancement of Unita's military capacity if things had gone to plan.

As Du Toit later recounted, his Special Forces unit had never in fact worked with Unita or had any liaison with the Angolan rebels. His was an operation 100 per cent made in South Africa. His group included two black former Angolans, who could have once been Unita, or more likely FNLA, who had been in the South African army since 1975. They were equipped with overalls like those of Gulf Oil employees and the plan was for them to try to take a prisoner from among the Gulf workers. They hoped to surprise someone off the base, alone, and to speak to him in Portuguese before tying him up and leaving him behind. After they left, the prisoner would be found by his fellow workers and would describe the 'Unita men' who had captured him. If the unfortunate prisoner should see any of the white commandos, however, he was to be killed. The plan, in order to pass off the sabotage as Unita's work, involved the Special Forces men carrying leaflets which claimed credit for the attack in Unita's name, a photo of Savimbi with the slogan, '1984, year of the anti-Cuban offensive', red paint for writing Unita slogans along the road and an old AK47 rifle on a rough piece of rope, to leave behind.

However, the plan began to unravel early the following morning when a patrol from the Angolan army (FAPLA) saw new footprints of boots on the edge of the forest and a new track through the high grass. The South African commandos had not known that there were no less than three FAPLA bases near the oil installations. At first assuming the tracks were those of Gulf workers who had been out hunting, the FAPLA patrol did not search deep in the forest, though Du Toit saw them come within 150 yards of his hiding place. But once the Angolan soldiers established that none of the Gulf employees had left the residential area during the night, they started a more careful search through the forest, and at one point an 11-man FAPLA patrol came within five yards of the South Africans. Late in the afternoon the patrol surprised Du Toit and his men by coming on them from an unexpected angle where they had no cover. The South Africans suddenly saw themselves surrounded. In the ensuing fire fight Du Toit split his men into three groups and retreated deep into the forest, hoping to be able to hold off his pursuers until dark fell and gave them back the advantage of surprise. Then the orders were to break through the FAPLA lines and flee towards Zaire. The original plan, which had given the men three nights to get back to the boats waiting on the coast, had envisaged a retreat to Zaire as a last resort. Once over the Zaire border their instructions were to head for Lake Luvulu and to make radio contact with South Africa. They would then be met by unspecified friends of South Africa in Zaire, as Du Toit put it, who would then take responsibility for them. But, although the other six escaped, the commander and his two colleagues never got the chance. Du Toit was captured, lucky to survive with serious wounds to his arm, neck and shoulder. His two companions were killed by the Angolan patrol.

Three weeks later, Du Toit, in hospital pyjamas with his shoulder and arm heavily plastered and the back of his neck still an angry red weal from its brush with a bullet, stood composed and articulate through an hour-long press conference. With the authoritative military manner of a young man used to command, and a pointer in hand, he showed on the maps on the wall behind him exactly where every step in his personal disaster had taken place.

To listen to him was to see young, white South Africa at its most pathetic – a highly trained young man who had spent seven years of his youth preparing himself to lead risky and illegal operations in countries across the region in defence of continued white supremacy in his own country. When Du Toit headed for Cabinda in his speed boat he was already a veteran of two similar acts of terrorism abroad from which the South African Special Forces had emerged unscathed. In 1982 he had been in one of several rubber dinghies launched off a South African destroyer into the mouth of Angola's Giraul river in the south of the country and had blown up the most important bridge in the province before being whisked back to South Africa in the mother ship. The operation was claimed by Unita, and the Angolan government's announcement of South African involvement made little or no international impact. In a similar operation launched from Durban, the target had been an ANC building which the South Africans blew up in the Mozambican capital, Maputo, without making any attempt to disavow it. The Western press barely reported incidents like these, and if they did, it was usually done from Johannesburg with the casual ideological and racial bias which characterised most of the regional reporting of that period and which contributed to the lack of international understanding of the undeclared war launched by South Africa across the region. Du Toit had plenty of time to reflect on the morality and the wisdom of his years of destruction in the Frontline States as he sat in prison in Luanda's steamy sea-level heat, reading the Bible and English poetry books which he had requested.

The implications of South Africa's direct involvement with Unita in an attack on a US company in which the lives of 128 US technicians were put at risk, brought an angry rebuke to Pretoria from the State Department in Washington. But 1985 was a year of dramatic infighting between different wings of the second-term Reagan administration, and the contradictions were on public show over policy in Southern Africa. Within days of the failed Cabinda attack, President Reagan in fact sent a message of support to a Unita-hosted international meeting of anti-communists in Jamba, organised and supported by a Republican millionaire from New York, Lewis Lehrman, who was running for mayor. 'Your struggle is our struggle,' read a letter signed by President Reagan but clearly bearing the hand of his Director of Communications, Pat Buchanan, and his ultra-right ally in the administration, William Casey, the CIA chief. The group Lehrman headed, Citizens for America, invited the Nicaraguan Contras, together with Afghan and Laotian rebel groups created and funded by the US, to the inaugural meeting of 'Democratic International'. The occasion, which had required a major CIA organisational effort of logistics, communications, press coverage and security handled through the South African military to get participants to the remote Jamba airstrip, was primarily a showcase for Savimbi to be presented as a democratic freedom fighter with an international profile.

Behind the scenes was another strand of US policy. In the ideological struggle nearer to home in Central America, Casey's CIA was busy stepping up clandestine supplies of equipment to the Contras in Nicaragua, and Soviet materiel captured by the South Africans in Angola provided a useful diversified supply. State Department officials were never told about these material links between the CIA and South African military intelligence chiefs. Savimbi, however, was the beneficiary of these relations, though he considered them no more than his due for a decade of harsh conditions in the Angolan bush which had been his fate after the Americans lost their nerve supporting the South Africans in the 1975 fighting.

The State Department repeated its censure of the SADF in June when, in another act of aggression against another Southern African country, they bombed what they said were ANC houses in Botswana's capital, Gaborone. But more important, and revelatory of Washington's increasingly strong-arm policy as far as Angola was concerned, were votes in Congress that fateful year. In June 1985 the US Senate voted to repeal the Clark Amendment and open the door to legal funding of Unita by a margin of 63 to 34, with 17 Democrats joining the Republican majority. A month later the House of Representatives also repealed the amendment by 236 votes to 185. In ten years the US attitude to Angola had come full circle, the shame of the mercenaries was forgotten, and the majority in Congress was ready once again to collude in a war of attrition against a civilian population waged for its own ideological reasons by South Africa for whom Savimbi was a convenient proxy.

The American administration of course chose to see things very differently and to overlook the implications of the Cabinda SADF operation and Du Toit's calm revelations of South African Special Forces posing as Unita in the most ambitious of sabotage operations. Nearly a decade later, in defence of the US policy he personally had done so much to craft, Chester Crocker was to write with reference to this period that 'Unita was a legitimate, nationalist movement – an indigenous phenomenon born of the grim realities of the Portuguese and Soviet-Cuban empires'. The great US theoretician of the region had access to all the information at the time which should have brought him to make a different assessment of Washington's most convenient ally, but no doubts or nuances were allowable as Crocker pressed on with the grand design for Southern Africa which was moving into a new stage post-Clark Amendment repeal. Crocker was the architect of Constructive Engagement, the US strategy to bring apartheid South Africa back from the brink of chaos. The plan was to build some respectability for Pretoria by the regime finally ceding Namibian independence and giving up it's long illegal military occupation. Crocker linked to this development a pull-out of Cuban troops from Angola – an American ideological goal, but presented to South Africa as a security measure for them.

The Angolan government promptly ended all diplomatic contacts with Washington, and the long-running and inconclusive negotiations over Namibian independence and Cuban troop withdrawal came to an abrupt halt which lasted 16 months. The right-wing ideological climate in Washington produced a tide of support for Savimbi which was curiously unaffected by the growing support for sanctions against his key ally, apartheid South Africa. As Frank Wisner, Crocker's deputy, put it harshly to Angola's Minister of Industry, Ismael Martins, in one of the exploratory informal talks over those months, it was 'important not to misinterpret the US sanctions debate or the unrest within South Africa ... the anti-apartheid sentiment in Washington was not a pro-Angolan sentiment; if anything, sanctions fervour on the American left had kindled the pro-Unita drive among moderates and conservatives'. The Angolan government was forced to recognise that they were up against even more implacable enemies in Washington than many of them had realised. The Reagan administration was, as Lucio Lara put it then, ' a catastrophe' for Southern Africa, and Angola's people were paying 'for all of Africa in the liberation of South Africa'. Joe Slovo, the veteran South African communist and leader of the ANC's fighters in Umkhonto wa Siswe, in Luanda that year thanked the Angolans for their generous 'shelter to liberation fighters for ten years' and sombrely assessed the price as 'hardly a day of peace ... mercenaries hired, bandit armies created, the economy sabotaged'.

Some clues to what lay behind the US determination to break the MPLA government could have been divined from the January policy-making conference of the MPLA in preparation for the Second Congress of the Party, to be held in December 1985. Angolans wore their ideology on their sleeve in those days. Addressing the conference, President Eduardo dos Santos underlined the themes of 'ideological unity and the Party's authority' to be discussed. In his speech to the Party he stressed that Marxism/Leninism was the MPLA's ideological base, and democratic centralism its organisational tool. He called on Party militants to guard the MPLA's ideological purity and strengthen discipline, unity and cohesion. To an outsider the image of discipline and cohesion in the Party was already striking. On international affairs the President announced that closer bilateral cooperation with all socialist countries was being studied, as was broader cooperation within the framework of Comecon. For the first time he said publicly that Cuba had decided a year ago to cease receiving payment from the Angolans. 'There is no material reward for the internationalism it practises in Angola in such an exemplary way in the military field.' He stressed too the important role of the Soviet Union in arms supplies and in a growing civilian cooperation. All of this ran precisely counter to what the Reagan administration wanted to hear, and set alarm bells ringing loudly.

Nor could the Washington of Ronald Reagan swallow this kind of ideology being taken for granted by the majority of Angolans, and even reinforced in practice daily. Almost every evening after work that year, in the pretty, bright blue, colonial building, half-hidden by flowering trees, which housed Angola's People's Assembly, Paulo Jorge, the former foreign minister, would sit for many hours with the 11 co-workers in his Party cell discussing the shape of the country's future. Other Central Committee members – none of whom could be cell coordinators – and Party officials spent similar evenings of study in workplaces and in villages all over the country. The MPLA-Workers' Party had 30,000 members, and for most of them 1985 was a year of long evenings after work drafting and redrafting a fat file of documents for the December Congress which was due to choose the country's leaders and policies for the coming years. Ordinary Angolans believed in their responsibilities and powers through the Party and were proud of the fact that, despite the strain of the war, Angola was trying to run contrary to the trend in Sub-Saharan Africa where the deepening economic and social crisis was pushing more countries towards anti-democratic personal rule. The Congress was to widen the Central Committee from 65

members to 90, and Lucio Lara, the Party's Organising Secretary
and the key figure behind the country-wide preparations, talked
early in the year of 'institutionalising a kind of people's power' so
that corruption, error and bureaucracy among the powerful could
be fought from the base. He was a man without cynicism and with
a boundless faith in ordinary people, whose constant travelling in
the remotest parts of the country had had a big impact and
maintained the credibility of the Party, already clearly under strain
as people's lives grew more difficult with every passing month. It
was a time when such gentleness from the powerful was met with
love from the powerless. Coupled with his legendary morality and
self-sacrifice since the war for independence, Lara's relentless
critique of South Africa and the United States for their backing of
Unita gave him an enormous popularity throughout the terrorised
towns and villages of Angola.

Other political trends in the Party were, however, pulling hard
in another direction that year. The trend which had used racism
to persuade the President to oust Paulo Jorge as Foreign Minister,
and which had seen Lucio Lara's wife and secretary and other historic
cadres excluded from the Party after an incident involving a satirical
painting presented for the President's birthday depicting a worldly
struggle between left and right, saw Lara dropped from the 13-man
Political Bureau at the Congress at the end of the year. It was a
barely hoped-for triumph for the Americans, made even more
welcome to Washington with the surprise down-grading at the
Congress of three other historic personalities from the liberation
war, all of whom were outspoken critics of US policy in Angola,
notably the support for Unita. Henrique Santos Onambwe, Minister
of Justice and Party Secretary for Judicial Affairs was dropped
from the Central Committee, Paulo Jorge and Air Force Commander
Iko Carreira became only alternate non-voting members. It was not
coincidence that all three were, like Lara, both mestiço and highly
educated. There were some among their enemies who referred to
them as 'the Algerians', a shorthand for the overtly radical orthodoxy
of the Algeria of Houari Boumedienne which had led the Third
World in the 1970s in the heady trials of strength with the developed
countries over the end of colonialism and then over oil prices. The
political group which had dominated Angola through the
independence war and the first decade of independence politics had
begun to lose its power to a new group for whom relations with
the West, and particularly the opening of diplomatic ties with
Washington, were priorities.

While this political drama was being played out behind closed
doors, the undeclared South African war against Angola went on
apace. The American determination to separate their reaction to
Pretoria's apartheid policies at home – which brought limited

sanctions in August – from Pretoria's impact on Angola through Savimbi, became clearer month by month. In September, while Luanda hosted the Non-Aligned Movement's ministerial meeting, a major offensive began in the remote bush in the east as the government tried to retake the little towns of Cazombo and Mavinga from Unita. After two weeks of heavy ground fighting, backed by upgraded air support and logistics from an Air Force re-equipped by the Soviet Union and reorganised by Colonel Carreira, Cazombo was recaptured by the government forces on 19 September. The town was ruined and desolate, its population long gone. It had been held by Unita for nearly two years. Lance-Corporal Hans Fidler, a South African doctor, was killed near Cazombo as South African air and ground forces intervened in an attempt to save Unita. The South Africans, who had made a show of withdrawing their occupying units from Angola on 17 April – albeit a year behind the schedule promised in Lusaka in 1984 – invaded again with commando teams. And 32 Battalion, the notorious unit formed from the FNLA and Unita deserters who fled south after independence in 1975, was brought in too in the attempt to save Mavinga for Unita. South Africa's Mirage fighter-bombers and Canberras strafed FAPLA columns and, in one incident at the end of the month, brought down six helicopters. There were a handful of survivors from the helicopter crews who gave a graphic picture of these grim encounters in the empty lands the Portuguese called 'the lands at the end of the earth'. One young sergeant walked for two weeks following the sun across a vast empty plain where he met not a single person and survived only because he stumbled on an abandoned Unita base where he found a jerrycan of water. Two lieutenants who walked 100 kilometres back to Cuito Cuanavale in five days of blazing hot days and freezing nights lost 25 pounds each in that inhospitable no man's land. One young officer described this new phase: 'the war has become routine to us – every day there is fighting, every day dying, every day prisoners, every day Unita boys giving up, every day peasants losing limbs and leaving their land.'

No one believed this haemorrhage of the country's youth and resources could go on. Daily the news from the front grew grimmer and the indifference of the rest of the world more incomprehensible to the Angolans under attack. The early days of October brought three major South African air attacks with hundreds of Angolans dead and wounded, a MIG21 shot down and dozens of trucks and armoured personnel carriers smashed out of action. The costs to Angola of the battle for Mavinga were estimated by a UN team as $36 million. South African Defence Minister Magnus Malan admitted publicly for the first time that Pretoria was giving Unita aid 'of a material, humanitarian and moral nature'. It was a sign of Unita's new and more respectable profile since the repeal

of the Clark Amendment and of South Africa's confidence that the
Du Toit incident had essentially done nothing to embarrass them
in the eyes of most of the outside world. Malan put a predictable
ideological slant on what the South Africans were doing, which could
have been written by Pat Buchanan. 'Through our connections with
Unita we maintain the interests of the free world on our sub-
continent,' he declared, and went on to say that South Africa
would break its links with Unita on condition that all foreign forces
were withdrawn from Angola. President Botha went further along
the same track: 'More Russians and Russian weaponry are being
employed to destroy the resistance of the Angolan people, just like
in Afghanistan ... in the light of all this, the government can hardly
sit still.' He urged the Cubans and the Russians to 'go home'.
Meanwhile, against the South African onslaught, the Angolans were
forced to spend almost half the budget on defence, and half a
million Angolans were in need of emergency food, the majority of
them displaced.

The fruits of South African aid to Unita were only too visible in
a rising tide of terrorism that autumn. Random death struck across
the country: a Catholic priest and nun killed by Unita while driving
patients to hospital in Cunene province; eight people blown up by
a bomb laid by Unita saboteurs on a Huambo street in the middle
of an ordinary day as people went about their civilian business. An
ambush of a government convoy in Benguela province killed four
senior provincial officials, and four more were captured by Unita.
Two weeks later ten Soviet military officials and eleven senior
FAPLA officers were killed when an Antonov was shot down near
Cuito Cuanavale by a South African plane.

And the South Africans had other techniques too. In September,
in a case as strikingly ambitious and illustrative of long-term
planning as Du Toit's failed raid, an elderly Portuguese citizen was
sentenced to death in Luanda for economic sabotage. Amilcar
Freira was a shipping agent from the port of Lobito. On holiday
in Portugal he was contacted by the South Africans and then went
to South Africa for two months. As he returned through Angolan
customs his sophisticated radio equipment attracted attention and
got him watched. The court case revealed how he had been radioing
to South African intelligence details of all ship movements in the
large port of Lobito. Based on his information an attempt had been
made to blow up a Cuban ship leaving Lobito for Luanda a year
before, but led to the sabotage instead of two other ships by South
African frogmen. In addition his South African-organised group,
which included four Angolans also in court, monitored all cargo
inputs at the port and their shipments up the Benguela railway.
The sabotage of the railway, which had left Huambo virtually cut

off except by air, was thus systematic and clearly orchestrated from Pretoria.

In late November Crocker met Savimbi in Zaire and invited him to visit Washington early in the New Year – the logical next step after the open recognition of their mutual interests which the year had brought. After a US visit in which Savimbi was treated with all the courtesies of a head of state, the Americans were ready to begin the covert aid to Unita planned since the rescinding of the Clark Amendment. Shoulder-held Stinger missiles, which could bring down helicopters and had been used by the American-backed fundamentalists against the Soviets in Afghanistan, and Tow anti-tank missiles, were among the first pieces of heavy hardware to be sent to Zaire for use in Angola from February 1986.

Even before the equipment could have actually arrived in Unita bases, the rebels put themselves in the forefront of the international consciousness by a mass kidnapping of foreigners. In March 1986 Unita kidnapped 150 foreign workers, including two Britons, in Andrada, a diamond-mining town in the northeast, and claimed to have seized 'kilos and kilos of diamonds'. Like previous groups of hostages, the men, the majority of them from Eastern Europe, were forced to walk through the bush for months before being freed in the Unita headquarters at Jamba. The hostage-taking roused little interest or indignation with Savimbi's backers, and meetings continued in various venues between Crocker and South African Foreign Minister Pik Botha to discuss the regional situation. The central question for them both remained how to put more pressure on the Angolan government to get the Cuban troops to leave. Savimbi himself visited South Africa in April and reiterated publicly his assurances from Pretoria that they would not consider pulling their troops out of Namibia until the Cubans had left Angola. Crocker's 'linkage' of the two issues had become routinely accepted as part of the regional picture.

Meanwhile on the military front, Unita, thanks to the new US equipment, was able to demonstrate new muscle. For the first time Savimbi was able to get to Munhango, in the centre of the country, indicating a serious deterioration in the government's position. President dos Santos flew to Moscow and received a warm pledge from President Mikhail Gorbachev that the Russians were ready to give further support to Angola in the face of the new level of aggression fired by the US boost to Savimbi. South African forces struck deep into Angola from Namibia, and in June South African frogmen hit the southern port of Namibe, attacking ships and oil storage tanks. A launch carrying Israeli-made Scorpion missiles entered the harbour at dawn and fired on three oil tankers serving the provincial capital. Two tanks were destroyed and one

damaged. Limpet mines were placed by frogmen on three ships in
the harbour, one was sunk and two damaged.

By the end of August, when the Non-Aligned Movement (NAM)
held its summit in the Zimbabwean capital Harare, Angola, and
Unita's new strength from its American backers, was high on an
agenda dominated by the question of apartheid South Africa and
its increasingly aggressive tactics at home and regionally. President
Robert Mugabe, in his keynote speech, made a stinging attack on
the Reagan administration, condemning Washington's military
assistance to Unita in their attempts to overthrow a legitimate
government. During the week of the summit the NAM leadership
was dramatically radicalised by the sense of South Africa's hidden
war conveyed by all the Frontline States' leaders. In the crisp
highland air of a Southern African spring, with the beauty of
dazzling purple, scarlet and pink flowering trees around it, there
was a shocking incongruity in the shattered shell of the ANC house
and office blown up by South African terrorism and left in ruins
in the centre of a city marked by a prosperity unique in the region.
The Zimbabweans wanted everyone to see it, from Rajiv Gandhi
and the Indonesians to the Yugoslavs and Latin Americans. That
grey rubble was part of what created the mood of anger and
defiance which had Fidel Castro, in his military uniform, cheered
to the roof of the conference hall as he denounced the Reagan
administration for its destruction in Nicaragua, its bombing of
Libya, its failure to condemn South Africa's war against the region,
and its arming of Savimbi in the attempt to force his troops out of
Angola. 'We will stay in Angola until the end of apartheid,' he
declared, to even louder applause. The Harare meeting ended
with a Special Declaration which committed every NAM member
to strict sanctions against apartheid South Africa, cutting air, sea,
cultural and sporting links, and to a boycott of South African
agricultural products, uranium, iron and steel.

In the immediate aftermath of Harare, and buoyed by the genuine
tide of moral indignation which was with them, the Frontline
States' presidents decided on a behind-the-scenes diplomatic
attempt simultaneously to detach Malawi and Zaire from their
supporting roles in South Africa's destruction of Mozambique and
Angola. In the weeks before the mysterious mid-October plane crash
in which President Samora Machel, on his way back from a summit
in Zambia, was killed on the South African border along with a
number of Mozambique's leading intellectuals and top officials, there
was a new tough spirit of determination in the region. And President
Machel's death did not end the initiative. Tanzania and Zimbabwe,
which control important access routes to Malawi, forced through
the signing of a defence pact between Mozambique and Malawi

in December 1986 which hindered South African access for the infiltration of Renamo guerrillas into Mozambique.

Equivalent pressures on Zaire were far more complicated because of its integration into wider US covert operations in Africa. The chosen vehicle for pressure was the Benguela railway. If the railway could have been reopened it would have meant increased economic cooperation between Zaire, Zambia and Angola. For Zaire it could have meant freedom from dependence on South Africa for the export of Shaba province's copper. But in fact all parties involved in discussions about reopening the Benguela line saw it as an opportunity for pursuing hidden and contradictory agendas. What for Angola was a way of neutralising Zaire's support for Unita was something very different for the European and US government and business interests, which backed the idea as a possible way of getting Luanda to negotiate security along the railway line with Unita, which controlled large stretches of it. The Americans were quite clear that for them the Benguela railway was 'a gambit', as Crocker himself put it later. He spelt it out openly in his 1993 memoir *High Noon in Southern Africa*.

> The beauty of the concept was that the railway would have appeal as a means of reducing the hinterland's dependence on South African-controlled transport routes for moving their foreign trade. Yet, since the railway passed through Unita-controlled areas, Savimbi's approval would be required. It might be a start to dialogue. US political support for Unita in key countries like Nigeria, Kenya, and Ivory Coast created yet another problem for the MPLA leadership to contend with.

Those three African countries, like Morocco and Zaire, so ready to fall in with US support for Unita and so unrelentingly hostile to Luanda, were indeed a serious problem for the Angolan government. US Secretary of State George Shultz had been on an African trip which had included these influential allies earlier in the year. The US goal of forcing the MPLA into reconciliation with Unita had been high on the agenda for talks everywhere. In April, President Denis Sassou Ngessou of Congo, fresh from a visit to Washington and anxious to please his hosts, invited Crocker to talks in his capital, Brazzaville, with an Angolan delegation to be headed by Minister Kito Rodrigues. But Kito's meeting with the Americans was something of a freelance initiative, unauthorised by the President, who was then out of the country, or by the Party. Kito's political star began to wane when news of the meeting with the Americans leaked out and he ceased to be the useful back channel to the President that Western officials had made him into. No progress came out of the Brazzaville meeting.

But President Mobutu was more than ready to play on the Americans' team in the Benguela game. On the twentieth anniversary of Zaire's sole political party, the Movement Populaire de la Revolution, in late May 1987, he claimed the project for his own, put forward 'in the name of my Frontline States' colleagues'. He went on to say 'the money is there, the only problem is one of security. Approaches had to be made to Unita to accept the neutralisation of the railway. We got that agreement. There is in fact a sort of indirect agreement between Unita and the MPLA to keep the line secure.'

There was no such agreement, hard though the Americans were pushing for it. However, in Lusaka the Angolans signed a joint communiqué with Zaire and Zambia which provided for the rehabilitation of the railway to go ahead on the understanding that it would not be used for military transport. Unita was quick to claim this as an effective cease-fire in a limited area and a capitulation under their military pressure.

In fact the fine fighting words of the Harare summit the previous year had done nothing to change the real situation of menace which Angola faced on the ground. US C130s, C141s, Hercules and Boeing 707 transport planes flew into Zaire from the US two or three times a week with arms supplies for Unita and the war was omnipresent. Since his open backing by the Americans, Savimbi was ever more confident of his diplomatic reception in many forums. So unembarrassed was he by his connection with the apartheid regime that he appeared alongside Chief Buthelezi in Capetown at the swearing in of the new minority South African government – a convenient appearance too for Crocker, who was then in the early days of trying to demonstrate that South Africa need not be a pariah in Africa. Savimbi, overnight the respectable face of African democracy, visited Europe and was received by right-wingers in the European parliament, and even unofficially by senior French officials.

In July 1987 Crocker visited Luanda in a mood as far from diplomacy and compromise as could be imagined. In two days of talks with the Angolans Crocker and his team put forward the suggestion of the Cuban contingent in the south leaving in a year, that in the north within three years, an African force replacing the Cubans, and a process of normalisation of US/Angolan relations to begin in parallel. When the Angolans raised the question of ending aid to Unita by the South Africans and the US, Crocker threatened that if the issue were raised, the South Africans would demand an end to Luanda's aid to the ANC while Washington would make Soviet support to the Angolan government part of the negotiations. The arrogant and dominating American tone, with Crocker making no secret of his scorn for the chief Angolan negotiator, Foreign

Minister Alfonso Van Dunem Mbinda, was then broadcast world-wide in a Worldnet television press conference in which Crocker described the Luanda talks as 'basically a waste of time'. His briefings to journalists that summer described Cuba and the Soviet Union as being, like Angola, determined to go for a military solution against Unita. This was vintage Crocker disinformation. Like everyone else involved, he knew how far advanced were the new and highly ambitious South African military preparations for a showdown on the battlefields of central Angola.

CHAPTER 4

Havana's Last Stand 1987–89

On 16 November 1987 in Havana the Cuban Central Committee made the dramatic decision to reinforce its 25,000 troops in Angola to counter a massive new South African commitment of infrastructure and logistics in northern Namibia which had begun in March. The South Africans, with the backing of the Reagan administraton, were preparing for the most ambitious offensive inside Angola since 1975. The Cubans' decision to counter it was equal in historical importance to the arrival of the first Cuban fighting contingent on 4 October 1975 which headed off the South African units bent on installing their client FNLA/Unita government in Luanda. The new decision flowed directly from Fidel Castro's defiant declaration at the Non-Aligned summit in Harare in 1986 that Cuba would 'remain in Angola until the end of apartheid' and his pledge in Havana earlier that year that Cuba was prepared to stay in Angola for 10, 20, or even 30 more years.

Castro had spoken in Harare against a regional background in which the Frontline States' morale was sinking as Pretoria escalated violence inside and outside South Africa. Mozambique was living through its most desperate military crisis ever, as Renamo units organised by the South African Defence Force and invading through Malawi sought to cut the country in half and take the coastal town of Quelimane. Two months later, the tension with South Africa culminated in the death of President Samora Machel in a mysterious plane crash at a remote spot near the Mozambican border but inside South Africa. A South African hand was suspected though never proved. At the same time three Southern African capitals were reeling from air attacks by the South Africans during the attempt at negotiations on South Africa's internal crisis by the Commonwealth Eminent Persons Group. Inside South Africa the State of Emergency was taking an unprecedented toll of anti-apartheid organisations, and the new weapon of vigilante violence had been unleashed by the state at the squatter settlement of Crossroads. Meanwhile Namibian independence was off the international agenda as Pretoria prepared its own Rhodesia-style UDI, and in Angola itself FAPLA government troops had not recovered from the serious losses sustained under South African bombing at Mavinga the previous autumn.

For the first time in the decade since independence, military leaders in the Frontline States were privately discussing the previously unthinkable possibility that the 'inevitable end of apartheid' might be much further off than they publicly predicted and that the sacrifices they and their peoples were making might not be short term. The private consensus of these men by late 1986 was that the white regime in Pretoria was preparing to escalate its attempts to break its neighbours and that other humiliating and ineffective Nkomati agreements, like Mozambique's, would become a new norm. 'We are involved in a war to the death – it's them or us,' said one senior official. In that context Zimbabwean and Tanzanian troops were fighting for the government in Mozambique, but a Cuban military presence in Angola 'until the end of apartheid' was the only real guarantee the region saw that Pretoria could be defeated in that life-and-death struggle.

South Africa chose to raise the stakes further in April 1987 with the improvement of its military infrastructure in northern Namibia, preparing for a major showdown in southern Angola which they were confident would go their way and pave the way to finally installing Savimbi in power and ousting the MPLA government. The South African generals aimed at the capture of the town and FAPLA base of Cuito Cuanavale, 200 miles from the Namibian border. This would give Unita a completely new strategic base to attack central Angola. Unita was then in a particularly confident phase, with attacks in the east and in new target areas in the north from US-aided facilities in Zaire increasingly catching FAPLA ill-prepared. This was in part because the Angolans were focusing their attention on the south and the reinforced South African presence. Through August and September South African units, numbering about 7,000 men, fought off a major FAPLA offensive in which they attempted, as they had unsuccessfully two years before, to retake the town of Mavinga, occupied by South Africa and Unita since 1980 and an important supply base for them. In mid-September FAPLA units were encircled on the Lomba river and took very high casualties. This was an important enough battle for the South African Defence Minister, Magnus Malan, for once to admit his troops' role in it, rather than pretending it was a Unita operation. He announced it as a victory against Russian and Cuban expansionism, although in fact only Angolan troops were involved against the SADF. Thanks to very active diplomacy by the Frontline States, in particular Tanzania, the United Nations twice condemned Pretoria's occupation and aggression, in November and December, but the South African military, convinced they were close to a decisive victory which would change the course of the war, pushed on towards Cuito Cuanavale unaffected by what the wider world might say.

But in the dry and desolate plains of southern Angola the military tide began to turn against them in the early weeks of 1988 with the arrival of the first additional 9,000 Cuban troops two months after the Central Committee decision. The shipment of the men and their equipment was a massive logistical exercise which absorbed the total attention of the Cuban leadership, including Fidel Castro himself, and brought back to Angola some of the generals who had been part of the 1975 campaign in Angola, and others who had fought in Ethiopia. The troops, who would number 15,000 when the deployment was complete, and their equipment, arrived at the three ports of Luanda, Lobito and Namibe and swept in three columns along the country's main west/east axes, from the coast to the mist, hills and forest of Malange in the north, to remote Luena near the border of Zaire and Zambia, and to the main war theatre of Cuito Cuanavale in the south of the country. In a country with Angola's broken infrastructure the relative smoothness of the deployments was a miracle. By mid-February these thousands of young Cubans were ready to take on the South Africans at Cuito Cuanavale in a set-piece battle of tanks and heavy artillery, including South Africa's mammoth G5 and G6 howitzers, aircraft, and anti-aircraft batteries. The Angolan/Cuban side, in which Swapo also fought, was led by the legendary General Arnaldo Ochoa Sanchez, an invincible heroic figure second only to Fidel Castro for the Cuban soldiers in the field. In the following weeks of heavy fighting they not only halted the South Africans, but defeated them so definitively that Cuito Cuanavale became a symbol across the continent that apartheid and its army were no longer invincible.

By early May the South Africans had been pushed back and the Angolan army was 50 miles east of Cuito Cuanavale. Fighting alongside the Angolans and Swapo, the Cubans fanned out south towards the Namibian border area, aiming to put an end to the years in which the South Africans had made the province of Cunene a virtual no-go area. The civilian population had long since scattered, their homes destroyed, their cattle stolen and driven south into Namibia, or used to feed South African soldiers. Ahead of the Cubans some South African units, together with the Namibian black conscripts who sometimes fought in Unita uniforms, retreated to the border area and in heavy fighting a dozen white South Africans were killed.

The Cuban-led campaign struck at the South African military's confidence and helped to set the scene for quadripartite negotiations which began in London in May with Angola, South Africa, Cuba and the US at the table. The central agenda items were the long-overdue independence of Namibia from South Africa, under the ten-year-old UN Resolution 435, and a timetable for Cuban withdrawal from Angola of its 40,000 troops. The Angolans raised the question of the end of aid to Unita being part of the agreement too, but Chester Crocker, US Assistant Secretary of State for African Affairs, spoke for Washington and for the South Africans when he said 'the question of our relationship to Unita is not a bargaining chip, we have no intention of ending our relationship with Unita'.

As the negotiations began in London, Cuban engineering units working round the clock under floodlights reinforced new forward air strips 40 miles from the Namibia border at Cahama and Xangongo with anti-aircraft weapons to protect the MIG23s and helicopter gunships newly in place there. The South Africans knew that for the first time they had lost air superiority to Angola's MIG23s, a fact which changed the military picture as dramatically as their defeat on the ground at Cuito Cuanavale. And thousands of South African troops were still inside Angola, in Cunene and Cuando Cubango provinces. The South African generals badly wanted to extricate them without humiliation and alive. They could not have known that the Cubans had already calculated that they could not afford to humiliate them as Reagan's Washington would have raised a hue and cry about the communist danger in the region and jeopardised the balance of the negotiations.

South African bravado, and a mistaken confidence in their diplomatic skills, led to an immediate attempt to outsmart the Angolans. Perhaps aiming to bypass the main negotiations, and in particular the shrewd Cuban diplomats on the team, the South African Minister of Defence, Magnus Malan, followed the London talks by setting up a meeting in Brazzaville with Angola only. With extraordinary hubris they offered a simple settlement 'between Africans' which would leave Namibian independence out of the picture and exchange a SADF withdrawal from Angola for a Cuban withdrawal and the expulsion of ANC guerrillas. A demilitarised zone along the Namibian border was also proposed. The echoes of Mozambique's 'non-aggression' pact with South Africa at Nkomati were too strong, and the proposed bargain held no attractions for the Angolans. For them Namibian independence had by then become the key incentive to any deal. Dr Crocker's 'linkage' could, they believed, finally be turned to the region's advantage.

Four-party talks began again in Cairo in June, but the atmosphere was immediately soured by the South African team producing a document which urged the inclusion of a reconciliation with Savimbi as part of the negotiation and a synchronisation of the withdrawals of the Cubans and the South Africans. Even the American delegation saw at once that this was too insulting to be considered as a serious negotiating position and overnight redrafted their allies' document to drop the references to reconciliation with Unita. Two days later, in a move which well illustrated the South

Africans' ambivalence about diplomacy versus military solutions, a South African unit guarding the Calueque dam on the Namibian border penetrated deep into Cunene province and killed more than 100 Cubans in a surprise engagement. The Cubans hit back with an airstrike which killed a dozen South Africans. There were still 1,500 South African soldiers 150 miles inside Angola in July, and in the military commanders' talks which were held intermittently in parallel with the main negotiations, the South Africans kept postponing their leaving date, despite the fact that they had originally promised to pull them out by the previous December. (They finally left in August 1988.) These demonstrations of lack of South African good faith put the negotiations under severe strain.

But it was not only the South Africans who were lacking good faith. The Americans dominated the negotiations themselves, but also set the political and military context in which they were taking place. During the negotiating period not only was Savimbi to go to the US on a high-profile influence-building mission, but the US military were in Zaire conducting joint manoeuvres with the Zairian army, code-named Flintlock 88, in which they would leave behind substantial amounts of equipment. The operation was a cover for equipping new northern bases for Unita as an alternative to Jamba and the southern infrastructure supplied from the South African bases in Namibia, in the event that the negotiations were successful and Namibia became independent. After the US manoeuvres finished near the Zaire/Angolan border on 12 May, Angolan intelligence identified six Unita training bases in Zaire as Kitona, Kincuso, Kimpese, Kahemba, Dilolo and, the most important, Kamina. During the manoeuvres an American Awacs reconnaissance plane patrolled along Angola's northern and eastern borders gathering information on Angolan military positions, according to Angolan intelligence. The Pentagon did not confirm either the intelligence gathering or the equipment brought into Zaire and left behind, but they did confirm that $50,000 worth of repairs were to be done at Kamina, an old Belgian base from the colonial days.

The Americans had been working secretly out of Kamina periodically in the previous year flying four or five missions a week into Angola. Unita prisoners and defectors had described the US pilots who flew supplies of explosives, anti-aircraft missiles and anti-tank missiles, in Hercules cargo planes, into Unita areas in eastern Angola, other US officers who supervised the strip lighting put down before planes landed, still others who worked with Unita officers sent to Kamina for training in intelligence and in the new weapons, such as shoulder-held Stingers, supplied by the Americans.

While the major military focus of late 1987 and early 1988 was on Cuito Cuanavale and the southern front, in the north 'Unita's American front' was building up fast. In the first half of 1988 60 per cent of Unita's offensive actions took place in a 150-mile band bordering southern Zaire, 600 miles north of Jamba, the traditional South African supply base. 'The Americans want to take away from Unita their negative image as puppets of apartheid,' said Lieutenant General Antonio dos Santos Franca, known as Ndalu, Angola's Chief of Staff of the armed forces and key negotiator.

Savimbi received $30 million support from the Americans in 1988, and besides the new military preparations being made for him through Zaire, diplomatic pressure increased behind the scenes on Luanda to bring him into a government of national reconciliation. This new demand was a prime example of the Americans constantly shifting the goal posts, hardening their attitude to the Angolan government. In contrast, as negotiations continued in Geneva, Brazzaville and New York between July and November, the Angolan/Cuban side made important concessions, judging the independence of Namibia, which would certainly bring their allies Swapo to power, to be the priority for the region. The new international climate too had begun to play a role, with the dramatic changes which would destroy the Soviet Union already casting an economic and political shadow over the continuation of the war to which they had contributed so much. The original proposal by Havana of a four-year wind down of Cuban forces was telescoped to 27 months. The Cuban military agreed to stay out of the southern area near the Namibian border; Swapo fighters too were to move north of the 16th Parallel in the transition period.

Even more significant, and indicative of the pressure they were under from Washington, was the Angolans' public declaration that the question of US support to Unita was not on the table any longer, as they had wanted initially in the London talks. In view of what was then going on militarily in Zaire and northern Angola this was an extremely risky diplomatic posture by the Angolans, forfeiting the kind of international support they had had during the South African invasion in late 1987, and obscuring the real state of their relations with the Americans and the real threat Unita posed. Behind this Angolan public position was of course the dream of normal diplomatic relations with Washington – the carrot always just out of reach, enticing them towards new concessions.

The end of South African support for Unita was, however, discussed behind the scenes, in parallel with a demand from South Africa for the closure of seven ANC training bases in Angola, which Luanda agreed to in the 13 July New York Principles. Ten thousand ANC fighters, who had played a defence role against Unita, began quietly to leave Angola for secret bases in Tanzania, Ethiopia and Uganda, or for the underground in South Africa, in the closing months of 1988. It was the end of an era of vital mutual solidarity in which Angola had provided the space for thousands and thousands of young ANC men and women, in flight from the repression of the apartheid government's State of Emergency, to train, to be educated, to consolidate a national political identity. The camps were tough places, constantly being infiltrated by the regime's agents provocateurs and with a large proportion of uneducated violent youths whose only thought was how to get back into South Africa as quickly as possible. Not all of them understood why they were involved in the war against Unita, but, whatever the resentments felt on that issue, some of their camps had been in key places and the loss was soon felt. The closure of the ANC camp near Malange in the north, for instance, came just as Unita stepped up operations in the province.

This attitude of concession on the Angolan side, together with the Reagan administration's anxiety for the beginning of a settlement on Cuban withdrawal before the November presidential elections, pushed the South Africans to the point where it became difficult for them to postpone the process of UN Resolution 435 on Namibian independence any further. The date of 1 November was set for the start of a seven-month process which would lead to elections under UN auspices in May 1989. Immediately thereafter the Republican George Bush was elected President of the United States in succession to Ronald Reagan just as the jigsaw of agreements were falling into place. Bush, as a former CIA chief from 1976, had old history with Zaire and plenty of experience of its suitability as a base for secret action in Angola.

On 22 December the New York Accords were signed between South Africa, Cuba, and Angola. Namibia was to become independent and the Cubans were to withdraw from Angola in stages over 27 months. The United Nations was to oversee the two processes. Both the Angolan and South African governments pledged to end support for each other's opponents: the ANC and Unita. The ANC announced in January that its bases in Angola were closed.

But any illusion that these dramatic changes in the regional landscape meant that life was to become easier for the Angolans swiftly vanished. It slowly became clear that all the compromises they had made were just the start of what was wanted by the Americans. When President dos Santos called in January for US recognition of his government, US Secretary of State George Schultz responded that normal diplomatic relations were out of the question until 'the process of national reconciliation was complete'. In February a new law offered amnesty to individual Unita members, but the Bush administration had more ambitious goals, involving Savimbi himself. Now that the Cubans had agreed to leave, it was the internal political future of Angola that was the focus of US attention. Chester Crocker was replaced by Herman Cohen and the goal of national reconciliation became the code phrase for getting their man into power. Savimbi and Unita, in the background throughout the eight months of international negotiations, moved smartly into the foreground.

Shorn of his all-important South African military support by the New York agreement, Savimbi might have been expected to be worried about his future, although the precedent in Mozambique where support continued to flow to Renamo after the Nkomati Accord, suggested that support might well continue. But the Americans let him know that 1989 was to be the year of increasing US support – no less than $50 million – in pursuit of the goal of getting Unita into power in Luanda. Serious human rights abuses by Unita in its hidden headquarters in Jamba were then coming into the open, but were ignored. And lest anyone should fail to understand how serious Washington was in backing for its protégé, two military supply flights a day began to come into Unita's areas from the military base at Kamina in Zaire. More US advisers were put into Kamina and within a few months the daily, or more often nightly, secret flights into Angola were increased to three. Kinshasa airport and Matadi port were in constant use by the Americans bringing in materials to ship on to Kamina. The American pretence that the shipments to Kinshasa were for the small war going on in Chad convinced no one. Zaire was once again the key conduit for US action in Angola.

In mid-March, with advice from his American backers, Savimbi offered to negotiate on a transitional government in which he would play no part, but Unita would be integrated into government structures. This was not seen as a serious offer in Luanda and was rejected. No one who knew Unita could imagine it at work without Savimbi. But the pressures for reconciliation increased over the following months. The former colonial power, Portugal, moved into a high diplomatic gear and talks between the MPLA and Unita were held under Portuguese auspices in April and June. At the same time American behind-the-scenes diplomacy began to draw in a number of African countries in the pressures on the MPLA as Crocker had earlier done. The most significant African player was of course Zaire, because of its key role in the war, followed by Gabon and Congo, with Côte D'Ivoire and Morocco also important because of their leaderships' ties with Savimbi. The two-year-old treaty binding Angola and Zaire to non-aggression, though not repudiated, was under severe strain in public and Zaire's effective repudiation of it was an open secret.

Suddenly the old alliances of 14 years earlier, in the run-up to Angola's independence, were back in action. On one side, backing the MPLA, the Namibian independence fighters of Swapo and the ANC, were the Frontline States, led by Tanzania's President Julius

Nyerere. On the other were the American allies. The Bush administration's policy had a double focus for them: to persuade the MPLA to find a space in power for Savimbi; and to accept the overtures of Pretoria, newly somewhat rehabilitated by the belated granting of Namibian independence and by the end of its part in the war in Angola, and with ambitions to be the region's, and then the continent's, economic and political leader.

In the unlikely setting of the marble halls and manicured gardens of President Mobutu's forest palace at Gbadolite on 22 June the US appeared finally to have succeeded in their Angolan plans. President dos Santos at last met Savimbi, in the presence of 18 African heads of state. After an awkward handshake, which neither of them wanted recorded on film, a cease-fire was announced and a peace deal, which involved Savimbi himself leaving the country for an interim period of two years, was announced between the two leaders. Unspecified 'privileges' for Savimbi were to be worked out in private. However, within two days, once the heads of state had all gone home, Savimbi denied that any such deal had been agreed. The war continued. Notes on the meeting at Gbadolite, taken by the Zambian President, Kenneth Kaunda, however, showed that the key to President dos Santos agreeing to a cease-fire had indeed been Savimbi's promise to remain out of politics for two years and to leave the country in return for an honorary title. The rest of the agreement concerned the cessation of South African and US aid to Unita, the integration of Unita cadres, and the maintenance of the Angolan constitution which was based on a one-party state. President Mobutu, who had his own reasons for wanting to please the Americans by pulling off a peace agreement, had been the go-between, telling President dos Santos that Savimbi had agreed to the two-year exit. Immediately after the meeting and before it was clear that it had fallen apart, Mobutu was received with great fanfare at the White House.

Within two months of Gbadolite Unita had launched 600 attacks across the country, and the government estimated that 733 civilians had been killed and more than a thousand wounded. In one incident Unita shot down an Antonov 26, killing 42 people. Meanwhile Unita officials increasingly raised the question of multi-party politics – a new focus of attention. Gbadolite, said Lucio Lara at the time, was used by Savimbi for propaganda purposes showing his readiness to negotiate, but without there being any intention on Unita's side of keeping to the bargain. Unita's military pressure on the government was matched by diplomatic gestures from the US such as the July vote in the International Monetary Fund on Angola's membership where Washington's was the sole vote against. During this period, as talks between the MPLA and Unita continued intermittently in Zaire and then in Portugal in August, September and November, the government made a key concession the Americans were looking for: they agreed to multi-party politics in return for Unita accepting a cease-fire and renouncing violence. In October, in response to Washington's pressures through the year and the fast-changing situation of the socialist camp internationally, the MPLA effectively abandoned Marxism as its theoretical basis and opted for democratic socialism.

CHAPTER 5

Losing the Peace 1991–92

On 31 May 1991, at Estoril in Portugal, in the presence of US Secretary of State James Baker, Soviet Foreign Minister Aleksandr Bessmertnykh, UN Secretary-General Perez de Cuellar and President Yoweri Museveni of Uganda representing the Organisation of African Unity, President dos Santos and Jonas Savimbi embraced publicly and signed the Bicesse Accord to end Angola's long post-independence war. It was symbolic of the balance of forces which had brought them to this moment that the two men differed so sharply in their manner: dos Santos was stiff and silent, Savimbi charming, exuberant, brimming with confidence, and ostentatiously deferring to dos Santos as 'my President'. Marrack Goulding, the UN's head of peace-keeping and a former British ambassador to Angola, watched the ceremony with a sense of foreboding for his old friends in the MPLA, sure, like all the Western observers, that they would not win the election set for the following year. James Baker had made the same calculation and told Goulding flatly that the US intended to keep up their funding for Unita so that Savimbi could campaign effectively. Such a continuation of open backing for their side by the US was entirely predictable and consistent with everything that successive US administrations had done since 1975. The long years of US military and diplomatic support for Savimbi's overthrow of the MPLA government had by no means come to an end with the peace treaty.

The signing of Bicesse came as both sides were exhausted. Although no one would have admitted it, since Cuito Cuanavale, the New York Accords of December 1988 and the stepped up US support to Unita through Zaire, the two armies were in a military stalemate which neither could see a way to break. Besides, the external forces which had driven the war in apartheid South Africa, and a Republican United States driven by Cold War preoccupations, which had fired the war, had, for different reasons, lost the incentive to be so directly involved. Bicesse was the culmination of ten years of American diplomacy deployed to end the MPLA's regime and to bring one of America's most important allies in Africa, Unita, to power. The final agreement took most people by surprise, but it reflected the dramatic changes in the region brought about by Dr Chester Crocker's policy of Constructive Engagement – and in particular the withdrawal of 50,000 Cuban troops from Angola in exchange for Namibian independence – and by the even more dramatic shift in geo-politics which had flowed from Mikhail Gorbachev's *glasnost* and the collapse of state socialist regimes across Eastern Europe. Neither of the old Cold War powers needed their African confrontation any more.

Bicesse provided for a cease-fire; the disarming and demobilising of both armies; the formation of a new national army with an equal number of soldiers from Unita and the government's FAPLA, under Portuguese and British instructors; and for multi-party elections which would be monitored by the UN.

Savimbi announced from Portugal that he would return to Luanda in a month, ready to participate in the Joint Political and Military Commission (JPMC) which was to have a monitoring role in the country in the 15- to-18 months proposed transitional period before the elections. The JPMC was to include delegates from the US, Soviet Union and Portugal – known as the Troika – the UN, the MPLA government, and Unita. It was to work by consensus. Like the peace settlement forced on Germany after World War I at Versailles, Bicesse was an agreement which set the scene for the continuation of the war by other means. And, like Versailles, this peace imposed by the stronger side (the US on behalf of its ally Unita) contained an implicit political humiliation of the weaker (the government of Angola). Those in the Angolan leadership who saw it in that light however chose not to say so, just as the Mozambique government, in similar circumstances in 1984 when they signed the humiliating Nkomati non-aggression pact with South Africa, presented it to their own people and to the outside world as a success. In both cases, as in a hall of distorting mirrors, the aggressor had become an equal party with the victim.

'No winners, no losers' was the stated principle of Bicesse. But in fact it was a triumph for the Americans who had by diplomacy successfully changed the balance of forces between the two parties, giving Unita the parallel legitimacy to the MPLA it had sought unsuccessfully on the battlefield since before independence, and undermining the sovereignty of the government. Bicesse deliberately left ambiguous the question of where real power was to lie in the transition period up to the elections. With the UN? With the Troika of US, Russian and Portuguese officials who had overseen the agreement? With the JPMC? With the Angolan government? Or with Unita's military force?

Two months before the signing, in a classic seizing of the media initiative by Unita, Savimbi, brimming with confidence and persuasive charm, held a breakfast party in an exclusive London hotel for half a dozen journalists. The coffee went cold and the scrambled eggs congealed as he revealed the outlines of an agreement so radically different from anything which had been proposed before that it was hard to believe one's ears. The key provisions involved such major concessions by the MPLA that some officials, hearing them for the first time from the press reports the following day, described them as either the usual Unita attempt to use the media to help create facts, or as a suicide act by the government. Most remarkable were three elements: the agreement to liquidate the government army, FAPLA; the ambiguous power relations between the JPMC and the government in the run-up to the election; and the imminent arrival of Savimbi himself in Luanda where the government had prepared a house for him. Reading the text of Bicesse in May it was clear that Savimbi in March had been correct in every detail.

Compared with previous peace proposals, notably the Gbadolite agreement of just two years before, made by dos Santos and Savimbi in front of half the heads of state of Africa and providing for the absorption of Unita's army into the FAPLA and for Savimbi to withdraw from Angolan politics for two years, Bicesse was a stunning defeat for the MPLA. Gbadolite was repudiated by Savimbi within a week because it effectively stripped him of the chance of power in the immediate future. Bicesse, however, gave him an even chance of political power in 15 months, and his advisers, particularly the Americans, persuaded him that it was a foregone conclusion that Unita would win the elections the following year. In addition, the agreement allowed him to keep his military forces intact inside a new army.

In 1991 all over the world socialist parties which had run one-party states, such as the MPLA, were being rejected by their people after years in power. Angola, most people believed, would surely follow the trend, leaving Savimbi as the beneficiary. The MPLA itself had already recognised the international trend and was in the throes of a complete mutation to try and ensure its future. In late March a congress of the formerly Marxist–Leninist party voted to change it into a social democrat party, broaden its membership and to form alliances with other new political forces.

Savimbi set his own return to Luanda for 1 July – a symbolic date immediately following the withdrawal of the last of the 100,000 Cuban troops which was due to be completed at the end of June. But before he started on the new phase of the power struggle in the open in Luanda with the MPLA he had unfinished business back in Jamba with his unacknowledged rivals, the Chingunji family. This dark side of Savimbi's life was one unimaginable to anyone who had seen only the suave, multi-lingual, persuasive Savimbi of Washington, Paris and London. Tito Chingunji had been a key figure in Unita's external relations in the 1980s. He had been the representative in Europe and in Washington and was responsible for much of the organisation's successful image making. But, like everyone else in his once powerful family, he had extremely ambiguous relations with Savimbi himself. On more than one occasion he asked Savimbi outright about the deaths of his parents and was always promised an investigation, though nothing was ever done to set one in motion. As though this challenge to the leader was not enough to keep him under a cloud, he fell severely out of favour and was in effective detention in Jamba for some months, when suspected of planning exploratory moves towards a negotiated settlement with the MPLA after the tide of war ebbed away from Unita in 1985.

Savimbi kept tight control over every family member. Tito's three sisters, Elena, Lulu, and Alice spent most of their time in Jamba's prison huts, though they were let out when Tito was in Jamba on a visit. Tito's wife was always kept in Jamba and never allowed to be with her husband when he lived abroad. Nor was Tito's nephew Dinho, son of the first chief of staff, allowed to spend any time with his uncle either when he was in Jamba for five months in 1986 or when he left to study. Dinho, whose first language was English from his childhood in the Unita refugee camps in Zambia, wanted passionately to go to the United States, where Tito was, but instead Savimbi sent him first to Portugal, then to London where the Unita office had instructions to watch him carefully. The shadows grew closer to Tito in 1986 when his brother in law, Wilson dos Santos, the movement's representative in Washington, was detained by Unita at their annual congress in Jamba as an American spy. Two years later Tito was finally sacked as Unita's foreign minister, recalled to Jamba, imprisoned and tortured. He was accused of witchcraft and of plotting to overthrow Savimbi. During the following year Unita several times denied publicly that Tito was under arrest, and during visits to Jamba by delegations of influential Unita supporters from abroad, including personal friends of the former foreign minister, he was produced to be seen, apparently free and part of Savimbi's entourage.

Misgivings over his fate, or that of Wilson dos Santos who had already been killed, together with his wife and family, did not, however, undermine US support for Savimbi during the critical years of the negotiations leading up to Bicesse. US Africa policy was so fixated on the need for a change from the MPLA government in Luanda that the issues of human rights and of democracy, to which the Americans paid so much lip service, were conveniently forgotten in the case of the killings, torture and holding family members as hostages which was going on in Jamba.

Post-Bicesse, in 1991, Savimbi's problem with Tito was that he could not allow him to be part of the group returning to Luanda to prepare for the elections. Tito's harrowing experiences of prison and torture in Jamba meant he knew too much about the realities of Unita far from the world of Washington lobbyists and diplomats. Also he knew too well too many influential people, particularly among the American officials. In just one day in Luanda he could have destroyed Savimbi's reputation irreparably and deeply embarrassed the Americans. However it was also unthinkable that if, as Unita claimed, Tito was free, he would not, as one of Unita's most experienced diplomats, be a key figure in the delegation in Luanda. So Tito was killed in Jamba. The news seeped out gradually among Unita's own cadres in the autumn of 1991 and was to lead, some months later, to the most important defections the movement had ever suffered.

Meanwhile all over Angola the new peace brought the reopening of roads which had been closed for years, a cautious start up for trading and businesses which had not been functioning because of the war, and the beginning of the return of Unita exiles from Portugal, Zambia or Namibia. The JPMC sat in Luanda to plan the organisation of elections in September 1992 and to set up cease-fire monitoring groups of both government and Unita officials all over the country. But the mood of cautious optimism that war had given way to politics was marred in many places by people's own experience of violent incidents. In January 1992, for instance, three British tourists and a New Zealander were killed at Quilengues, a Unita area 90 miles from the southern town of Lubango in Huila province. Huila is a rich farming province, but sparsely populated with few towns and much woodland. There was no government administration in the area the tourists passed through and just off the road was a Unita assembly point for troops waiting for demobilisation. Their three-vehicle convoy was stopped at a Unita checkpoint at dusk and the first car was sprayed with bullets while the two tourists in the second car were summarily executed, according to a peasant who witnessed the ambush. The bodies were later found 300 yards from the Unita camp. The third car managed to get away and alert UN personnel who rescued one wounded survivor from the first car. The bodies were stripped and the cars ransacked. It was five days before Unita allowed police to visit the scene and 19 days before UNAVEM arrived to launch an investigation. The UN team took a long time to report and its report was then officially inconclusive, although UN officials concerned had no doubts that Unita soldiers were responsible. There was a chaotic and unconvincing attempt by Unita to frame a slightly mentally disturbed peasant named Celestini Sapalo. Nevertheless, the British ambassador in Luanda, the Western diplomat most closely involved with the incident, said privately that the UN investigation was not clear and suggested the four were killed by bandits, or even by deserters from the government army.

The incident was one of dozens which would never be resolved in the confusion and vacuum of power of the next months in the run-up to the election. But Quilengues was the beginning of serious questioning of UN impartiality which would dog the organisation's credibility throughout the year up to the election at the end of September 1992.

From many towns and villages reports came into the JPMC of armed Unita men in civilian clothes moving in, or of arms caches being buried. Government officials in provincial towns were buried alive, burned to death or shot. In the corridors and waiting rooms of MPLA officials in the multi-storey Party building in Luanda groups of men and women in shabby clothes with tired, anxious faces came from miles away and waited to see Party officials to tell their individual stories of Unita's 'pilot committees'. Their stories were frightening and horribly consistent. These committees were groups of men in civilian clothes but with an unmistakably military air who moved into towns or the outlying shanty towns of the capital, bringing an atmosphere of intimidation, and who were frequently seen moving heavy boxes believed to be arms. Everywhere a palpable tension was growing among Angolans.

The tension turned to fear in February when two of Unita's top generals who were part of the diplomatic negotiating team in Luanda defected and sought political asylum in Portugal. Antonio da Costa Fernandes and Miguel Nzau Puna had been close to Savimbi for 30 years and were frequently the public face of Unita shown abroad. But the news of the killing of Tito Chingunji in the autumn of 1991, and their fear that Savimbi was preparing to exonerate himself for it by blaming Puna as Unita's 'Minister of the Interior', was the trigger for their dramatic change of camp. The two men came from Cabinda province in the north and had always therefore been on the outside of much of the internecine war in Jamba among Savimbi's own people from Bié. Both men knew many top US officials so well that they expected their revelations that Savimbi had a 20,000-man secret army in reserve which he was not going to demobilise, and was preparing to return to war if he did not win the election, to be treated seriously. 'I don't want to responsible for what is going to happen,' said Puna. The two men intended to set up a new political party, to be, as they put it, the real Unita, one which could appeal to all those who wanted a new political start for the country. The Americans took them seriously enough to get the International Committee of the Red Cross to take Costa Fernandes' children out of Jamba within three days, but not seriously enough to consider dropping support for Savimbi and putting their weight behind a new leadership of opposition to the MPLA. Fernandes was bitterly disillusioned by his old friends and allies in Washington. But the long years of personal involvement between Savimbi himself and a generation of Africa policy makers in Washington outweighed any misgivings some officials may have developed about the implications of what was now well known about his human rights record for the future of Angola. Besides, so sure were the Americans that he would be in power in six months' time that they had no interest in the fresh light on the situation offered by Fernandes and Puna which merely destabilised their plans.

Angolans, however, drew their conclusions from the defections rapidly enough. In March an emotional mass meeting in a stadium in Luanda saw the launch of the 'MPLA's Big Family' and the welcome back into the party of some of the Party's significant figures ousted in the infighting of earlier years for which some had paid a bitter price of prison sentences. A spontaneous revival of the Party began all over the country. At every social level militants became active again after five years or so of doldrums and disillusion, and people were prepared to drop everything to work for the MPLA in a collective throwback to the mood of 1975. MPLA stickers mushroomed on dogs' backs and babies' nappies. 'After all the disappointments, all the ridiculous follies of the leadership in the last few years we still have to give them one more chance: we'll give all our energies up to the election, but then we'll see about launching a new party,' said one former prominent MPLA member. Much of the impetus came from sheer fear of what it would mean were Unita to come to power – a reality being spelled out before their eyes daily by Unita behaviour in the towns and by Savimbi's far from conciliatory speeches.

The United Nations' Secretary-General's Special Representative for Angola, Margaret Anstee, arrived in Luanda at the end of March to find she was heading an operation which was months behind schedule and showing every sign of being undermined by Unita's flagrant defiance of her officials in much of the rural areas and provincial towns. Miss Anstee had been a highly placed UN official in the bureaucracy of Vienna. She had no personal experience of Angola's history and was heavily influenced by the UN in New York, and in Luanda by the British ambassador, John Flynn, and by the bullying senior US official in the JPMC, Jeffrey Millington.

The gravity of the situation was not presented to her as a moment for stark choices of how to confront Unita's cavalier disregard of so many of Bicesse's provisions. Worst of all, Unita remained in control of 24 municipalities and 162 communes and showed no sign of returning them to government administration as required by Bicesse. Just before her arrival, Nigeria's Major-General E. U. Unimna, head of the UN's military monitoring mission in Angola (UNAVEM) spoke for the world body about the Unita areas such as Jamba: 'If there is no opening up there will be no electoral registration, and no registration means no election – there can be no moral justification for this.' The Minister for Territorial Administration, Lopo do Nascimento, who was in charge of preparing for the election by extending the government's administration throughout the country, said the same thing as Miss Anstee arrived: 'We need to set a date for the elections and then put a final date on extending territorial administration so that we can start registration. Where we cannot register, we cannot have elections.'

However, such clear cut positions disappeared quietly in the next few weeks and the cynicism of the international community's commitment to the actual conduct of the elections began to show. A visiting American official, Jeffrey Davidow, even suggested that the election should be held without any registration, as it was clear that time was short and the logistics of organising registration were extraordinarily difficult given the country's broken transport infrastructure and the need for training a completely inexperienced group of officials to do it. The MPLA angrily rejected that suggestion, but failed to get the UN to take seriously the grave political implications of effectively conceding to Unita the control over Jamba, much of Bié province, and a substantial area of the north. Between them the Americans and the UN decided that the issue of lack of government control over a great swathe of the country was too difficult to resolve and simply allowed Unita to remain in effective control of its areas and thus in control of both registration and, eventually, voting. At that stage it would not have been impossible to resolve if the international community had had the political will to demand Unita's compliance with Bicesse, but it suited the Americans well to allow Savimbi the extra insurance of continuing control over his own areas, and it was a sign to the MPLA not to demand too much.

Lopo de Nascimento, trying to explain that this unresolved issue of control would make a mockery of elections, said, 'Unita has a totalitarian conception – they can not accept that where they are there could be other opinions'. But the UN and the rest of the international community chose to ignore such warnings. They even ignored them when they came from men whose whole life had been in Unita and for whom leaving the organisation was a personal tragedy (unlike Costa Fernandes and Puna who were important enough to have their future well looked after). Captain Abel Joao Cogi was one of the dozens of obscure Unita officials who defected to the government in this period in the full and terrible knowledge that he was thus condemning his wife and three children to death in Jamba.

Cogi was part of the Unita delegation to the cease-fire monitoring commission in the eastern town of Luena. It was his home town

and his mother still lived there, but Cogi obeyed the standard
Unita rule that no member of a delegation could have any contact
with local people or with MPLA officials. For weeks he sat at the
negotiating table opposite a woman who was his cousin. He never
spoke to her. But after some time local people who had known him
years before began to bring him small presents of food and household
goods when they saw that the Unita delegation had no money for
the smallest necessities and was poorly lodged in one of the many
buildings semi-destroyed by the Unita offensive just before the 1991
cease-fire. Luena had been one of the towns targeted in a last-
minute attempt to extend rebel control. But the gifts were reported
to Unita security and Captain Cogi was ordered by the head of his
delegation to return to Jamba and told he was under suspicion. 'Four
others from various delegations – a general, a major, and two
captains – had already had this happen to them. After they were
recalled to Jamba they were never seen again, and no one knows
what happened to their families either. I was desperate,' Cogi
explained later. Under tight MPLA security protection in Luanda
weeks later Cogi still feared for his life. 'They've sent people here
who know me and one day they'll get me. But I won't have died
for nothing if I've managed to tell people outside what Unita really
is – a dictatorship.' However, no one with any power was listening
to him, any more than they had listened to Costa Fernandes
and Puna.

The key provisions of Bicesse for holding the elections in the very
short time of 15 months were, besides the return of the whole country
to the administration of the government, demobilisation of the two
armies and the formation of the new national army. By the time
Captain Cogi was vainly trying to get a hearing for what he knew,
and perhaps gain a sudden international notoriety which might even
save his family, all three provisions were looking like something from
another era. There were those who thought that the arrival of Miss
Anstee might transform the process by a high-level UN refusal to
allow Unita's systematic breaking of the accords to continue, but
they were rapidly disillusioned as the UN continued to act as
though everything was on track as planned. And when in April US
Assistant Secretary for African Affairs, Herman Cohen, visited
Luanda he reinforced the decision to focus on the technical
difficulties, minimise them, and ignore the political implications.
At this time Unita occupied about one fifth of the country, had
refused to surrender any heavy weapons and consistently brought
into the demobilisation camps mainly young boys and older men
who were clearly not the real Unita army, and the formation of the
new government army was months behind schedule. Cohen even
suggested that the possible non-existence of the unified army by

the time of the elections in September would be no bar to the elections being free and fair.

Events on the ground showed how very far from realistic that was. Savimbi's rallies, often shown on television to the whole country, had become scenes of rabid incitement to civil disobedience. Several more foreigners had been killed, including a Portuguese former law lecturer in Luanda, Pinto Ribeiro, with his wife and children, and harassment of MPLA officials as well as ordinary citizens was endemic throughout the country. In Benguela's sister port city of Lobito there were a series of attempts by Unita to take over buildings which were prevented by a determined confrontation by the Provincial Governor, former Foreign Minister Paulo Jorge. In the capital no firm action was taken by the government and heavily armed Unita soldiers were openly on the streets in the Miramar area around Savimbi's house which was in a road of embassy villas.

During voter registration in July and August, brigades of school teachers and civil servants were sent all over the country by the government. They registered 4.8 million people, surpassing by far the hopes of the UN technocrats who organised the exercise. But records of local reports to the independent National Electoral Commission showed in eight provinces a chilling pattern of Unita disruption of the registration, kidnapping of officials, stealing of the electoral register, burning of cars, flight of the local administration, the holding of a UN official for 24 hours, and other violent incidents which brought the local officials in numerous cases, to request the cancellation of the register. None of this was considered by the UN or the National Electoral Commission as information which should have been in the public domain, nor as a shadow over the election. Herman Cohen and his officials, in Washington however were kept well informed by close contact with the Director of Elections, Onofre dos Santos, a member of the Central Committee of the National Liberation Front of Angola (FNLA), the CIA's old client from pre-independence days.

In a serious miscalculation of the political impact this violence would have on the future, the government, like the UN, chose not to publicise these violations. Nor, after the resignation of Lopo de Nascimento as Minister for Territorial Administration in April, was the fundamental question posed of how the election could be run in the one fifth of the country controlled by Unita and mostly off limits to any outsiders. (The Minister who succeeded do Nascimento foolishly even said publicly that the whole country was under government control, thus allowing the question to be dismissed.) Ministry of Home Affairs figures showed an administrative vacuum in eleven provinces. The UN technical team, taking their cue from Miss Anstee that the elections would go ahead however bizarre the circumstances, violated Bicesse's provisions by flying into Unita territory in a UN plane, taking an MPLA official in with them, overseeing registration, and flying out again, taking the official with them for his own safety. No canvassing by other parties – neither the MPLA or the small third force parties – was conceivable in these places. There were many reports of Unita officials collecting up all registration cards and saying they would be handed back on election day. Meanwhile tension rose with a Unita communiqué in August which threatened that the party might not accept the results of the elections, claiming that 500,000 people had not been registered. At the same time a secret Unita arms depot containing a tonne of war materiel was discovered and fighting broke out between Unita and MPLA supporters, notably in Malange in the north where several people were killed. In Lobito, during Unita's August congress, 900 armed men took over the port.

In the week before the election in late September, peace hung by a thread after a series of incidents such as one when Unita men burnt three cars in the President's motorcade during a visit to Bié province, seized ten policemen guarding President dos Santos, and took over the airport for the day. The next day in Huambo, ahead of the President's arrival on a campaigning trip, Unita fighters left one of their camps at dawn in five armoured personnel cars and headed for the airport, and a police patrol was dispatched to head them off. A clash was avoided by swift intervention by the MPLA and Unita regional commanders. To the great alarm of UN officials Savimbi said publicly that if he lost the election he would not accept it. In several apparently hysterical speeches he threatened whites and mestiços, said journalists would have their legs cut off, and that the police could dig their own graves.

By then only 10 per cent of Unita troops had been demobilised and 47,000 remained within the UN supervised camps as organised, disciplined units, despite clearly not being the best of Unita's troops. In addition, all Unita's heavy equipment was still intact and had not been turned over to the UN as the agreement provided. 'The international community is very short-sighted in not recognising publicly that this cannot be a fair election when one side, Unita, is a military force in control of about a fifth of the countryside,' said one UN official. At the same time, almost every day unrest broke out in one or another of the government's demobilisation camps where the FAPLA soldiers were desperate to get home, but had not been given their demobilisation kits and were increasingly restive and often hungry. They left their camps and set up chaotic road blocks, UN personnel and journalists were taken hostage in the camps on several occasions, and ugly scenes of hand to hand fighting and intimidation took place on air strips where hungry, penniless men had waited for days or even weeks for a chance to board a plane for Luanda. Only about 40 per cent of FAPLA soldiers were actually demobilised and at least 55,000 were in limbo, unpaid and roaming the country. The government was overwhelmed by the organisational task and incapable of mastering the situation. The UN's World Food Programme office saved the situation from serious anarchy by an extraordinarily efficient logistics operation and by courageous flights by its director, Philippe Borel, into the worst crises which he successfully defused.

Campaigning ended two days before the election with Luanda brought to a halt by rival motorcades through the city. Under the thousands of billboards devised by the Brazilian public relations firm employed by the government which showed President dos Santos with the promise of 'A tranquil future', MPLA banners across the road saying 'Make Angola a garden of love' and the Unita slogan 'Dr Savimbi, symbol of unity, dignity, identity', the whole city was on the streets. Horns hooted, commandeered buses and trucks were packed to the roof by people waving the black, red and green flags of Unita, or the red and black flags with a yellow star of the MPLA. T-shirts and caps of the rivals sprouted everywhere, from the middle class suburbs to the poorest shanty towns. But under the flowering trees in the Miramar suburb tension around Savimbi's house grew, one of the embassies was taken over by Unita soldiers, shooting incidents multiplied, the approach road was filled with heavily armed Unita soldiers, and some diplomats left their homes for the safety of a hotel, while a minister living nearby stopped going home.

On the first of the two election days people started to queue at the 5,800 polling stations in schools and government buildings before dawn. They were to vote twice – for one of the eleven candidates for President and then for Party candidates for the 230-seat National Assembly. Ninety per cent of those registered turned out to vote, often walking many miles and waiting for many hours in the sun for their chance. In the main towns most polling stations had half a dozen representatives of the parties sitting observing the poll. Eight hundred foreign observers were spread out across the country. In the port town of Benguela, one of the hot-seats of tension, officials, showing their position by a piece of yellow string around their arms, searched everyone for arms. Electoral officials, mainly school teachers and civil servants who had volunteered for the job, showed great commitment and faith in the process. Many stayed as long as three or four days in remote places sleeping at the polling stations through the two days of voting and then until the boxes were collected.

As voting got under way that first day, the Governor of Benguela province gave a formal lunch for some of the foreign observers. The long table in his palace was covered with the crispest of white linen cloths, sets of crystal wine glasses and heavy silver – Portuguese colonialism's leftover trappings. After the soup, an enormous fish was served, then a heavy pudding and coffee, with all the formal protocol Europe's worst colonial power managed to pass on with independence. The youngest person at the table then tapped his glass for silence and, like a well-trained minor royal, made a polite little speech of thanks to the Governor for his hospitality and time on such a busy day. Michael Kennedy, the amiable younger son of Bobby Kennedy, who has interests in the oil industry, continued his speech with an optimistic projection for Angola's future after the day's historic and successful election process which had, he said, closed the chapter on nearly 30 years of war. Governor Paulo Jorge was looking down at his small, neatly manicured hands, his face expressionless.

Chaos and tension began soon after the orderly poll. The UN computers suffered a power failure and much of the UN logistics broke down in the regions. Despite the promise by the Director of Elections, Onofre dos Santos, that first results would be available within hours of the polls closing, a vacuum of official results allowed Unita to start claiming victory on its radio station before dawn on the day after the election. A Unita spokesman accused the national radio of issuing false figures in order to provoke Unita and ordered party members not to listen. The national radio and television had dispatched 6,000 people to cover every polling station and as the counting finished in each one they sent their reports to the radio headquarters in Luanda. Unofficial reports poured out of the radio and television hours or even days ahead of the results from the National Electoral Commission (CNE). Although every result was signed for at the polling station by its official representative, Unita headquarters in Luanda repeatedly claimed fraud. The process was greatly delayed as the CNE bent the electoral rules to allow Unita to verify the independent body's work. No frauds were discovered, but that did not stop a Unita assault on the credibility of the election, nor its threats of war if the results were made public.

During a week of acute tension the UN accepted the Unita blackmail and did not release the results. Provisional results showed dos Santos with just over 50 per cent and Savimbi with 39 per cent in the presidential race; in the National Assembly the MPLA scored better with 55 per cent against Unita's 33 per cent. Drama mounted rapidly, though UN officials, with an extraordinary determination not to face the facts, were still desperately trying to play it down. At a hastily convened midnight press conference Unita's General, Arlindo Chenda Pena, announced that he and other generals were withdrawing from the fledgling new national army. Only a week before the generals had been sworn in to command the new Angolan Armed Forces (FAA) and had declared the fusion of the two former enemy forces was 'irreversible'. The next day

Savimbi fled secretly to Luanda airport and took off for Huambo. Late that night in the heavily guarded radio building a weary Lopo do Nasciminto, the MPLA official in charge of the election results, was sitting among the empty coffee cups in the MPLA's strategy room where the still incomplete results were being analysed. 'If he's gone to Huambo it is a declaration of war,' he said. Others did not want to see things that way. Yet again the key players in Washington and the UN decided to give Unita another chance to play by the rules of politics, ignoring the evidence on the ground that the rebel movement had a very different agenda. In Washington Herman Cohen said 'there is still time and still grounds for optimism'.

CHAPTER 6

Another Somalia ... the War of the Cities 1992–94

In the first week of October, with the results of the election still not announced, Savimbi silent in Huambo, and a mood of acute anxiety mounting by the day in Luanda, Western diplomats and UN Secretary-General Boutros Boutros Ghali for the first time began to talk about the possibility of changing Angola's constitution in order to create the post of Vice-President for Savimbi. To the Angolan leadership it was a quite extraordinary response to the dramatic new political situation inexorably unfolding, From 6 October radio and fax messages began to come in to the government from four provinces of Unita attacks by soldiers coming out of the demobilisation camps weapons in hand. In Luanda itself Unita blocked access to several neighbourhoods. For months before the election Governor Paulo Jorge in Benguela and a handful of other MPLA leaders had been warning that week after week there were complaints from peasants living near demobilisation camps of incidents with Unita soldiers coming out of the camps, heavily armed in contravention of the UN rules, and extorting food or beating people up. Suddenly it was on a different scale. From Uige and Bié in the Central Highlands and from Moxico in the east came reports from MPLA local officials of attempts by heavily armed Unita soldiers to kill or kidnap them and the police. In Zaire province in the north, MPLA officials were forced to flee from Nzete, in Mbanza Congo town the governor's palace was encircled by Unita fighters and the oil town of Soyo was occupied by them. Although the information was sketchy there was no longer any possible doubt that the often repeated threat by Savimbi to return to war was actually being carried out.

No one could say they had not been warned. On 3 October Savimbi broadcast a 'Message to the Angolan Nation' on the Unita radio station 'Voice of the Black Cockerel' which, though in his classic convoluted and contradictory style, was without doubt a clear repudiation of the elections and an attack on the electoral commission.

It is a pity for me to tell you that the MPLA wants to cling to power illegally, tooth and nail, by stealing ballot boxes, beating up and deviating poll list delegates, and distorting facts and numbers through its radio and television network. I appeal to all the Angolan people to remain serene. I appeal to all Unita militants to remain vigilant as in the past. At the right time we will give an adequate response to the MPLA manoeuvre.

He also urged Unita militants to 'accomplish the orientation that he or she has received'. The immediate reaction of Angolans who heard the speech was acute foreboding that the period of politics and elections was definitively over and the return to war was imminent.

But the UN, still preoccupied with getting the results of the election out and dealing with a welter of new technical complaints from Unita officials, failed to raise the alarm about what was happening elsewhere in the country or to warn Savimbi that grave repercussions could be expected from such defiance of the international community. Perhaps it was just too early for them to face the enormity of the failure of their own unfinished work. The demobilisation camps which the UN had overseen all year had served Unita well. Their troops had had a respite from the harshness of life in the bush and been fed, clothed and given medical attention by international aid agencies while remaining as intact military units. Those who had surrendered weapons knew that they were stored in the camp and, with a change in the wind, could be reclaimed. Meanwhile the military units of their MPLA enemies had largely disintegrated. In many places there was still utter confusion as the men voted with their feet and headed for home with or without formal demobilisation, while many officers had long since left the camps ahead of their men in the rush to get into business. From the centre the MPLA government, despite their misgivings about Savimbi's intentions, had made a genuine attempt to demobilise honestly to comply with the Bicesse agreement in the hopes of finally winning the international respectability and US diplomatic recognition which had eluded them for so many years. Reliance on the electoral route mapped out by the international community now came close to losing them power altogether.

The most influential Western diplomats in Luanda had apparently believed their own confident propaganda in the months before the polls that Savimbi would win, based partly on their lack of regard for the MPLA and also on the assumption that the Ovimbundu, being the largest ethnic group, would give Unita victory in what they saw as an election which would be decided mainly on an ethnic basis. They were stunned, first by the election results which appeared from the UN's estimate to give a narrow victory to President dos Santos, second by the Unita leader's hasty departure to Huambo, and then by his subsequent refusal for days to speak to them even on the telephone. When contact was finally re-established by satellite telephone, the diplomats of the Troika, Portugal, the US and Russia, with the South African foreign minister Pik Botha, and Miss Anstee, flew repeatedly to Huambo. In long meetings in his 'White House' they tried unsuccessfully to persuade Savimbi publicly to accept the election results, to agree to negotiations on a second round of presidential elections (as President dos Santos' final score was just under 50 per cent), and to agree to a meeting with President dos Santos. Their focus was still on the elections and none of them chose to confront him with international outrage at his decision to resort to war.

Mr Botha's intervention confused the situation yet further as he tried to set up a parallel negotiation to that of the Troika and the UN, pressing the idea of an interim government of national unity as a face-saving device for his old ally, Savimbi. These outsiders' hubris that they were still in ultimate control of the situation played into Savimbi's reckless determination to use whatever level of force he could to take power and his belief that he could do so with impunity. Tension built up in the capital every day as the population waited to see who would break the political stalemate, and how.

The election results were formally announced on 17 October. President dos Santos had won 49.57 per cent of the votes for the presidency, compared with Savimbi's 40.07 per cent – a result which meant a second round must be held as no one had a clear majority. In the legislative elections the MPLA won 53.74 per cent, giving them 129 seats, while Unita won 34.10 per cent and 70 seats. None of the small parties got even 3 per cent of the vote. Belatedly, on 19 October, the US endorsed the elections as 'generally free and fair' and urged a run-off for the presidency be organised as soon as possible. But it was far too late to hope for that, as the Americans should have known. That very day the long-planned summit between dos Santos and Savimbi was due to take place in Luanda and in anticipation of the Unita leader's arrival from Huambo Pik Botha and the US Under-Secretary for Africa, Herman Cohen, stationed themselves at Luanda airport to meet him. After five hours in which messages went back and forth to Huambo in response to a new demand from Savimbi that the meeting be held at the airport instead of at the presidential palace at Futungo, the two diplomats gave up the wait, belatedly realising that it was fruitless. All that was salvaged from these high-powered international interventions was an agreement by both sides that two commissions, one political and one military, would be set up to keep a dialogue going which, it was hoped, would eventually produce the meeting between the two leaders on which such hopes were being placed.

One mid-October dawn Luanda was shaken by explosions as Unita blew up a huge arms depot near Luanda airport and the UN headquarters, causing panic in the capital. Other arms depots, under UN custody according to Bicesse, in Bié, Huambo, Cuando Cubango and Moxico were also blown up, under the noses of the UN officers stationed in these places. It was a foretaste of much worse to come.

By the last week of the month, in a dramatic reversal of the pre-election situation, more than a third of the country was in Unita hands. In almost every province hundreds of small towns lived through the trauma of seeing their administration seized by rebels, police killed and government officials fleeing. Some days as many as a dozen municipalities changed hands as the MPLA struggled with a virtual vacuum of power and minimal military backing. Unita harnessed the confusion in many places by its old tactics of intimidation and terror. Witnesses reported bands of stone-throwing children converging on state administration buildings or police posts, backed by hundreds of men armed with machetes and sticks, while Unita troops armed with rifles, grenades and bazookas moved in behind them. In one incident two policemen, reluctant to fire on children, were burned alive. Unita troops from the demobilisation camps had moved seamlessly back into the war mode, just as Generals Costa Fernandes and Puna had forecast they would eight months before.

In the first sign of a tough verbal response from the government the three governors of the embattled provinces of Benguela, Huila and Luanda together on national radio warned Unita that they would accept no more encroachments on territory. However, the brave words had nothing behind them. The situation was militarily and politically out of control and deteriorating fast. Meanwhile the two commissions began to meet from 22 October, and the Unita generals in the military commission, including General Ben Ben, in a bewildering touch, appeared again in their FAA uniforms, allowing the international observers a moment of optimism. As Miss Anstee put it, 'We clutch at symbols, if not at straws, in our search for a positive outcome.' But the meetings of the two commissions and of the JPMC (the Joint Political Military Commission) in those late October days were punctuated with such outbursts of rage and accusations of election rigging from Unita officials, notably their delegation leader Salupeto Pena, that no coherent negotiations on the various proposals put forward ever took place. UN officials described Salupeto Pena as not quite sane, or a man possessed, in some of his shouting scenes, and suspected that drink and drugs were playing a part in setting the scene for the endlessly postponed series of meetings in the drab Joint Commission building in central Luanda.

Meanwhile, the situation outside the capital became ever more grave with Unita starting to take control of Angola's second city,

Huambo in the Central Highlands, where Savimbi had been holed up in his White House on the edge of town since it became clear he had lost the elections. Two days of heavy fighting between Unita forces and police backed by former government soldiers who individually joined the defence of the town, ended with the senior MPLA official forced to flee. Dozens of people died in street fighting as Unita took over the radio station and the hospital. A week before, as though to underline their effective control in the city, some of the MPLA's most prominent supporters, Professor Fernando Marcelino, his wife Miete, who also worked at the university, and his sister Dilar, a religious lay worker, were murdered by Unita in an ambush outside their friend David Bernardino's house. Within weeks Dr Bernardino was gunned down too. These murders were intended to intimidate the population and were highly effective. They were a demonstration that even the best known, the best educated, the most loved of local leaders, and whites, were not strong enough to protect themselves against Unita. They showed the population too that no one in the UN or the international community could or would protect anyone against Unita either.

Unita's defiance of the international community was paying off. On 29 October in Washington, Herman Cohen criticised the Angolan government for 'its seeming winner-take-all post-election attitude and the confrontational posture of its police force which exacerbated tension'. He went on to say that both sides were refusing national reconciliation. This was a positively Orwellian presentation of reality with a clear political message to Savimbi that the Americans were still backing him despite everything. Unita by then controlled more than 70 municipalities and held military positions in eight of the eighteen provinces. And in fact dozens of policemen had been killed by Unita in the month since the polls, and the police restraint under provocation was noted by many observers. At the same time President dos Santos had made repeated overtures of reconciliation to Savimbi, who had turned them all down.

The very next night after Cohen had spoken, Luanda itself became the scene of heavy fighting. Unita troops moved on the city from three directions, tanks and truckloads of soldiers drove through outlying suburbs, firing wildly and sending people dashing to hide indoors. Meanwhile the armed Unita pilot committees, which had been a menacing presence within the capital since well before the election, staged attacks on the airport, several police stations, the MPLA party building and the radio station. There were simultaneous attacks in the towns of Huambo, where three government officials were seized by Unita, and in the diamond mining centre of Cafunfo, in Ndalatando, Lubango and Lobito.

The government had no FAPLA to call on in extremis, and only a fledgling national army, who were not called out. They had to rely on the riot police, the so-called ninjas, who Unita had so often asked to be disbanded, to protect the population. The attacks by Unita pilot committees inside the city were widely expected by both government and population, as the pilot committees had been seen to be stockpiling arms in dozens of cases and had been openly aggressive in their neighbourhoods for months, and especially since the election. In the last days of the month the government had distributed arms to MPLA civilians and to former FAPLA soldiers to defend their neighbourhoods. Unita had at least 3,000 troops in the capital in addition to the well armed pilot committees. The rebels' plan, revealed in documents in the handwriting of Salupeto Pena, and other Unita leaders which were published later by the government, was to take advantage of the rising tension to create chaos and fighting on the streets, assassinate MPLA leaders whose names they had on lists, and use the opportunity to negotiate a political settlement which would efface the humiliation of the lost election. MPLA activists mobilised themselves to defend the capital, just as they had in 1975 when the FNLA had attempted to take it over.

On the Saturday afternoon, following a particularly acrimonious morning meeting of the Joint Commission, Unita attacked a police station in the centre of the city opposite the Hotel Turismo, fighting broke out in many places across the city, and Unita began taking hostages in the embassy district of Miramar where their own headquarters was a heavily armed camp. Among them was David Chambers, the British head of a major company and his Bulgarian-born wife, seized at gun-point from the empty Swedish embassy where they had been hiding, and the Zimbabwean ambassador, Dr Neville Ndondo. Most embassies had already evacuated their staff to hotels. The US compound was surrounded by Unita troops, some of whom climbed in and tried to get some Americans to go with them to Savimbi's house, just a block away, where they were keeping the other foreigners. In the house were the top Unita leaders, Ben Ben, Chitunda, Chivukuvuku, and Salupeto Pena, who was drinking heavily and conducting increasingly hysterical conversations on a walkie-talkie with the MPLA's General Ndalu. In mid-afternoon the government's General Carneiro returned to the JPMC building still hoping to continue the acrimonious meeting of the morning and persuade the Unita leadership to calm their people, but no Unita officials ever arrived.

Later in the first of the three days of the battle for Luanda, Herman Cohen got through by satellite phone to Savimbi's house in Miramar and tried to speak to Salupeto Pena as the most influential Unita leader still in Luanda, as well as the closest to his uncle, Savimbi, and most likely to be in touch with him. But the other Unita officials would not at first bring Salupeto Pena to the phone because he was in such a state. Chitunda's diary, found later when Savimbi's house was entered by government supporters, recorded both Salupeto Pena's drinking and Cohen's warnings that Unita should not take US hostages. 'The US government can be of more help if the Americans are left where they are and not touched by Unita.' The other foreign hostages would, Chitunda believed, save the leadership from being bombarded by government forces.

From the relative safety of the British embassy, where a lunch had been planned bringing together officials from both sides and where she had been trapped by the fighting, Miss Anstee was in frenzied contact by satellite phone with New York and London. The priority was to make contact with Savimbi himself. After many hours of trying, the British ambassador, John Flynn, got through to him during the night and spoke on behalf of Miss Anstee, with whom Savimbi's relations were then very cool. Flynn spent a surreal hour trying to bring the Unita leader to discuss a cease-fire and a return to the negotiations. Miss Anstee kept a note of the conversation in which Savimbi ranged from Munich and Churchill, through the impossibility of living under mulattos, to dos Santos being from Sao Tome, not Angola, to Savimbi having told Nasser to steal Jewish territory, and to his determination to resign if Bush did not win the US election the following week. Again and again he reverted to the safety of his nephews, Salupeto Pena and General Ben Ben and his own lack of a future if they should be killed in the fighting in Luanda.

The following day fighting continued around the two main hotels in the centre which housed Unita personnel, the Turismo and the Tropico, and Miss Anstee tried, unsuccessfully, with the Red Cross, to organise the evacuation of several dozen women and some severely wounded people. Chaos and desperation mounted across the city. Two Unita generals, Makevala Mackenzie and Zacarias Mundombe, disassociated themselves from what Unita was doing and surrendered to the government. At Miramar, Salupeto Pena urged his people to leave Savimbi's house and hide wherever they could in private houses or in one of the nearby embassies. He believed that the army was closing in on them with tanks, though in fact Unita controlled the whole district except for the US compound, and the US military were making emergency preparations for a possible evacuation of their personnel if any of them were taken hostage. The four Unita leaders split into two pairs to leave the headquarters, Chitunda with Chivukuvuku, and Savimbi's two nephews, Salupeto Pena and Ben Ben, together. The first two hid in a small room of a deserted house belonging to the US oil company Chevron. Ben Ben, after calling the MPLA's

General Carneiro at midday and talking about organising a cease-fire, turned off his phone, got in a car with Salupeto Pena, and Mr Chambers and his wife. They planned to make a break through the roadblocks and leave Luanda for Caxito, the first town on the road north of the capital and then in Unita hands. Caxito, capital of Bengo province and 50 kilometres from Luanda and key to all road links to the north and northeast, was occupied by General Numa's Unita forces preparing a stranglehold on the capital. One of the two brothers, Salupeto Pena, was killed in the next few hours, though Ben Ben had a miraculous escape and eventually reached Unita lines at Caxito. When Chivukuvuku and Chitunda a few hours later also opted to try to get to Caxito, their car did not get through the first of the roadblocks and Chitunda was killed outright. His bodyguard then shot himself in the head, according to Chivukuvuku's account. Chivukuvuku himself was badly wounded in the legs, but was taken to a police station after he was found hiding in a house by government militants. He was given protection by top army officers and taken to hospital.

Hundreds, perhaps several thousands, of people died in street fighting over three days which left Luanda traumatised. To the horror of many MPLA supporters hundreds of young men given guns as protection used them in revenge attacks on supposed Unita supporters and even on Zairians suspected of supporting Unita. 'For the first time I saw that we too were capable of the same brutalities we had seen Unita perpetrate over the years – our side had lost its special quality,' said one university teacher later. Many Luandans hid Zairian or Ovimbundo colleagues, fearing for their lives if they should be taken for Unita supporters. These were essentially political killings not 'ethnic cleansing', there were no cases of killing of prominent Ovimbundus. A Roman Catholic priest, Father Adelino Simoes, who worked in the Luanda suburb of Viana, wrote to the local administrator a month later detailing murders of named Unita supporters whose killers were known to local people. 'The panic among the Umbundu people was enormous ... some had to sleep outside their homes.' The priest described how he had pleaded with the police, and even with the administrator himself, to stop the manhunts. 'Everything that occurred is a heinous crime, because everything was committed in the open air, with "protection". Those that went around hunting the adversary were doing so triumphantly, in the plain light of day, and they remain unpunished,' he wrote, echoing the university teacher's agonised realisation. The repeated appeals from the government on the radio to the people not to take reprisals for the Unita attacks went unheeded in the powder keg of emotion. Killings by supporters of both sides continued after the three days of fighting and spread way beyond the capital.

In the wake of Unita's apparent coup attempt and the chaotic settling of scores which followed, the country was in shock. The international community signally failed to rise to the occasion – only Norway, which sent 33 doctors and a field hospital to Luanda, made a response which matched the depths of the immediate practical need. Many UN officials saw clearly that in those three days in Luanda, months of work on organising an election which, though flawed, did represent the will of the people, had been destroyed. But the UN leadership was conspicuous in the weakness of its public response.

Despite the defeat in Luanda and the four other main towns where the Unita attacks were concentrated, rebel units were still on the move in the countryside, and in the following days troops consolidated their hold over two more provincial capitals, Caxito, only 35 miles outside Luanda, and Ndalatando in Kwanza Norte. Desperation was mounting in the UN as they watched all central control unravelling. Miss Anstee and a senior UN official sent in from New York, former British ambassador to Luanda, Marrack Goulding, spent days being kept waiting for a meeting with Savimbi, finally flying to Huambo at the end of the first week of November. The two were taken by Unita to a night meeting in a grim and grimy building miles into the countryside where, in a surreal scene, Savimbi sat, surrounded by his top advisers, under shelves and shelves of blonde plastic dolls, and treated the two Westerners to a marathon ramble across the history of the Roman and Persian empires, through De Gaulle and Churchill, to the deaths of his nephew and Chitunda. The only things to emerge clearly from the meeting were Savimbi's reluctance to meet President dos Santos, and his inability, or unwillingness, to discuss any concrete plan to stop the fighting across the country.

Back in Luanda the next day the UN officials, still clinging to the hope that the Bicesse process could be brought back to life, pressed New York for an enlarged UN role and continued trying to talk to Savimbi by satellite phone and to get his formal acceptance of the election results. Savimbi himself meanwhile made a rapid visit to Zaire to talk to the Cabinda separatist movement FLEC. It was yet another clear sign of Unita's preparations for pressing on with the military solution.

But the UN continued to try to organise peace talks. In the first of a series of abortive meetings which were to try even the UN patience to the limit, government and Unita delegations met in the southern coast town of Namibe on 26 November and agreed to a cease-fire. It was the first of the meaningless negotiations which bought time for Savimbi. Two days later Unita took over the highland town of Uige and the air base of Negage, which had for years been the nerve centre of the MPLA's air defences against the

South Africans. UN Secretary-General Boutros Boutros Ghali belatedly reported to the Security Council that the situation had undergone 'a catastrophic deterioration'.

The lightening Unita offensive which pushed the government out of nearly two thirds of the country in three months was only possible as a well-planned operation prepared months in advance – as Costa Fernandes and Puna had revealed at the beginning of the year. It depended too on a vast re-supply and logistics operation from South Africa, then in the dying days of apartheid, but with enough of Savimbi's old associates in positions where they could still help him. In addition it was supported by units of the Zairian army deployed by President Mobutu fighting alongside Unita. Dozens of supply flights from South Africa into Unita-controlled airstrips were monitored by Frontline States, and a network of former South African Defence Force personnel working as mercenaries were flown in. The capture of the diamond mines at Cafunfo provided Unita with significant resources which paid not only the South Africans and Zairians, but also for arms suppliers from many other countries.

The MPLA was utterly stunned by the speed of the reverse and unable to rouse any part of the international community, even the Frontline States, to make an effective response, even on the diplomatic front. The coalition of forces against the MPLA in 1992 was essentially a rerun of the struggle for power in the run-up to independence 1975, and the international indifference to what was happening illustrated how little the hostility to Angola's government had changed despite the end of the Cold War and the MPLA's winning of the election. The reasons for this lay deep in the roots of US bureaucracies and intelligence services and the careers of a generation of high-fliers such as Chester Crocker, which had been for so long intertwined with Savimbi and the myth of his democratic credentials.

Over Christmas 1992, with the Unita offensive in full swing, towns and municipalities fell daily and Unita soon occupied two thirds of municipalities. The government army was largely dependent on local volunteers to hold the line. The UN then finally moved onto the diplomatic offensive, but in a way which was ominous for the Angolan government and was to compound the tragedy unfolding. Mr Boutros Ghali offered to host a meeting between President dos Santos and Savimbi in New York or Geneva. The proposal – for a head of state to travel abroad to meet the leader of a rebellion against him – illustrated the grotesque position of the UN on the new war: that both sides were to blame and had the same legitimate concerns. In a travesty of justice, the elections, judged free and fair by the UN, and the new multi-party government announced in December, had not fundamentally altered the international community's attitude towards the MPLA. Unita and the South Africans used the vacuum of power in Washington between Bill Clinton's election and inauguration to step up a new war to reverse the results of the election the UN had been so proud of. There was only silence from the outside world.

The War of the Cities

Angolans were plunged into an unimaginable hell. The economic and agricultural base of the country was smashed in the first three months of the Unita offensive. The high hopes which drove the brief return to normality of the early months of 1992 vanished for everyone in the closing weeks of the year. The UN estimated at the beginning of January 1993 that 10,000 people had been killed since the election. Three million people, including tens of thousands of lost or abandoned children, were on the move in flight from Unita, a tidal wave of hunger and misery which washed up either in the violent, overcrowded streets of Luanda or in makeshift refugee camps completely lacking resources. In Unita-held areas radio and telephone communications were cut. The only information to reach the capital came slowly with those who managed to flee on foot with chilling stories of the terror of forced dislocation, of brutality, of hunger and of lack of medical care for the many wounded.

In January 1993 Unita pushed into the whole diamond mining area in the northeast, took the oil town of Soyo which accounted for one third of the country's oil revenues, and seized the strategic airport of Cuito Cuanavale. They attacked 10 out of 18 provincial capitals. In a second attempt to take Benguela they infiltrated into the town before being repulsed in street fighting by a force which was entirely police and volunteer former soldiers, led by the Governor Paulo Jorge. Then, having thus failed on the coast, Savimbi's generals changed tack and brought a 10,000 man army up to the Central Highlands city of Huambo where Savimbi had been living since October. On 8 January they began to shell the beautiful city of flowering trees, old colonial squares, and industries which had restarted in the brief window of pre-election peace, with tanks and heavy artillery. Government planes bombed the rebels, flattened Savimbi's White House and added to the civilian casualties too. It was the most important battle of the new war and Unita threw into it the crucial aid from Zaire and South Africa. A hundred-strong force of mercenaries drawn from among former South African soldiers were recruited by the security consultancy, Executive Outcomes, and brought in to the battle for Huambo. A network of small companies based in South Africa flew the men and military supplies clandestinely into the Gove airstrip 40 miles from Huambo, and flew the wounded out to hospital in Namibia and South Africa. The siege of Huambo went on for 55 days. The city's inhabitants dug underground bunkers and lived on stored rations under a rattle of artillery which never stopped. The small garrison and police were joined by everyone able to hold a rifle. Virtually every building in the city was pock-marked with bullet holes, and many were reduced to rubble. The wounded and dying lay in the streets for days with no one able to help them, electricity failed, clean water ran out, and Unita refused all access to the Red Cross and UN agencies. Philippe Borel of the World Food Programme appealed for a brief truce for aid flights to be allowed into Huambo after an estimated 10,000 civilians had died and 100,000 people had fled the city. One journalist left behind, William Tonet, describing the horrendous scenes of decomposing bodies said words failed him: 'You have to see it to believe it.' Throughout February government relief columns for the tiny garrison struggled up from the coast towns of Benguela and Lobito, but made achingly slow progress as Unita had blown all the bridges on the main road. On 7 March, before the column could arrive, Huambo fell to Unita. The government soldiers withdrew from the city with a vast column of 100,000 men, women and children who started a harrowing three-week walk to the government-held areas on the coast. It was a journey the weakest, such as the women who gave birth on the way, did not survive. Hundreds, or thousands, died of exhaustion and malnutrition, others were swept away and drowned as they tried to cross the rivers with no remaining bridges.

With the capture of Huambo, Unita controlled five provincial capitals – prizes undreamed of during the long years of the South African war of the 1980s. Beyond Caxito the other three towns were in the north, Uige, Ndalatando and Mbanza Congo. Savimbi, receiving journalists flown in to Huambo through Zaire, told them his forces were poised to take four more in the centre and the east which were then under siege: Cuito, Malange, Luena and Menongue. Days and weeks of artillery barrages reduced much of these towns to rubble and the population to living in bunkers, to eating rats, and to creeping at night through the minefields which ringed the towns to fields where they could find food. Day after day casualties, mainly women and often children, mounted from land mine accidents which blew off feet or legs at a rate which soon made Angola the grim holder of the world record for mine victims, eclipsing the better known dramas of Cambodia and Afghanistan. Without medicines, water, or electricity, desperately undernourished victims of mines or shelling perished in great numbers. In Cuito, where not a building was left intact, the dead were buried in mass graves in the town squares which before had been playgrounds. The Angolan military dropped supplies by air to all four towns which helped hold starvation at bay, but often started small-scale fighting as soldiers from both sides fought for the drop. Only the military radio contact with headquarters provided a tenuous link to a world where normal life still went on. The horror of how life had been reduced to a numb battle for survival in these towns was unimaginable to everyone else, and those among the MPLA leadership who never forgot it for a moment paid a heavy psychological price as they agonised without being able to do anything. In all the years of South African invasions, Unita offensives, destruction of villages and crops, kidnapping of youth, nothing like this new war of the cities had ever hit Angola.

Savimbi's threats to extend his control area, and the scale of human suffering they promised, made no apparent impact on the outside world which had ceased to focus on Angola since the failure of the election.

It was to take the failure of two rounds of UN sponsored peace talks outside the country, starting in Addis Ababa in January and Abijan in April, before the Clinton administration finally decided on recognition of the beleaguered multi-party government whose legitimacy was disputed by no one except Savimbi. Some in the new Democrat administration appeared more prepared to abandon Unita than their predecessors. As early as mid-February some of Clinton's advisers proposed putting an ultimatum to Savimbi to return to talks or see Unita declared outside the law and the international community ready to support the government and lift the Triple Zero provision which, since Bicesse, had prohibited arms imports to either side. However they backed away from such decisive action within days and Ambassador Walker, the Americans' second man at the UN, announced that the US had 'no plans to recognise any party at this stage'. There were many in the UN and elsewhere at that time who believed that Unita might well win the war, and censure from the international community would then have produced an embarrassing problem. It was a repeat of the old calculation about overlooking Unita's behaviour before the election because they were expected to win, and again it bought time for Unita to pursue the military option.

The Addis Ababa talks in February 1993 were a classic demonstration of the Unita double agenda. 'We came prepared to sign a cease-fire immediately ... but the Unita delegation did not show the minimum interest in accepting peace,' said the government's negotiator, General Higino Carneiro. The UN finally called the talks off at the end of February after the Unita delegation leaders failed even to appear in the Ethiopian capital for a second round. Their public excuse was that it was too dangerous for them to leave Huambo because of government control of the air, though safety guarantees were promised by the government and endorsed by the UN. In fact the delegation was in the Zairian capital of Kinshasa throughout the negotiations, playing for time while they consolidated their position on the battlefield.

President dos Santos, against the background of the horrors going on in the besieged cities, requested immediate sanctions on Unita, freezing their assets and bank accounts and stopping their travel facilities. But, particularly after the fall of Huambo which made it appear even more possible that Unita might win this war, the international community held back from action, though the Security Council did at last strongly condemn Unita's violations of the peace accords and demand a cease-fire and the resumption of dialogue.

Another marathon of talks began in Abidjan in April. Côte D'Ivoire had been chosen in part because of the aged President Houphouet-Boigny's long personal relationship with Savimbi. In the deepening grimness of Angola everyone was concerned to do whatever was necessary for easy communications with Unita in the hope of avoiding any repetition of the non-event in Addis Ababa.

But Unita's firing on UN planes in Uige and Luena just as the talks began did not bode well. And as the weeks wore on the Unita delegation, in between displays of extreme bonhomie with the government delegation and many delays while they waited for instructions from Savimbi, eventually put forward power-sharing proposals, but refused to withdraw their troops from the occupied towns and cities as the quid pro quo. Both sides agreed to an expansion of the UN role from the current 75 military observers and 30 police observers, but Unita insisted blue helmet peace-keeping forces must be on the ground before they could sign a cease-fire – a proposition which the UN could not accept, despite enormous efforts by Miss Anstee to persuade New York that this could be the critical detail which would change the course of Angolan history.

As the talks dragged on, the urgency of a settlement was brought home to the UN itself when another of their planes carrying food aid was hit by a Unita ground to air missile outside Luena. The Russian pilot managed a crash landing, but it was in one of the minefields that Unita had laid down to maintain the town in a state of siege. The five man crew was badly injured, but there was no doctor or medical supplies in Luena and no facilities for night landing for a rescue plane from Luanda, so they spent the night in the minefield, with one man dying and another losing both legs.

With the months of sieges which virtually destroyed the towns of Cuito, Luena, Malange and Menongue, Unita intended to build on the capture of Huambo by an effective partition of the country.

This would create the conditions to force the government to accept, and the international community to endorse, a power-sharing arrangement in which Unita's military position, not its electoral score, would be the determining factor. Unita was then proposing an equal share of Ministers and provincial Governors, an integrated army and police, and joint control of the media. Bicesse – which had been such a good deal for Unita only two years before – was a dead letter, overtaken by a military campaign which the UN failed to anticipate.

In June the Clinton administration finally lifted its arms embargo against the government of national unity, sworn in in March and with five positions reserved for Unita, plus Army Chief of Staff and Deputy Chief of the General Staff. During these three months UN planes continued to be shot at, UN staff killed, UN equipment stolen, and access denied to vast areas of the country, but none of this humiliation of the world body changed the policy of placating the killers.

Miss Anstee was replaced as UN Special Representative on 28 June by the former Foreign Minister of Mali, Alioune Blondin Beye, who, from his first visit to Huambo in early July, reported some optimism for re-launching peace negotiations. Beye was an affable, confident figure who found it easy to be on good terms with everyone. His optimism would become his trademark through the coming months of continuing war and failing negotiations. On the diplomatic front, encouraged by him, African states such as Morocco, Sao Tome, Côte D'Ivoire, and even the president of the African National Congress, Nelson Mandela, were drawn into an attempt to organise a meeting between President dos Santos and Savimbi. In April the ANC's Thabo Mbeki had visited the leaders of two of Savimbi's close African allies, Côte D'Ivoire and Morocco, to discuss the fast deteriorating situation in Angola. Later, Mr Mandela , on a stop-over in Rabat after the Organisation of African Unity summit in Cairo, proposed a meeting for September for the two Angolan leaders under the auspices of King Hassan of Morocco. The ANC presented the proposal as an OAU initiative, though the Secretary-General of the OAU, Salim Ahmed Salim, said the organisation was not involved. The OAU's only attempt to mediate had failed in late 1992 just as the war was getting underway, when a mission led by the Zimbabwean president, Robert Mugabe, had travelled to Luanda. Savimbi would not leave Huambo to meet the delegation and, in marked contrast to the UN, South African, and US delegations who flew repeatedly to Huambo to see him, the OAU team refused to accept the demand to see the Unita leader in his own fiefdom. But in the intervening seven months of open war there had been a sea change in international attitudes to the Angolan conflict and the reluctance to confront Savimbi had even spread to such former close allies of the MPLA as the ANC.

Nelson Mandela's own determination to make reconciliation work in South Africa, his description of Frederick De Klerk as 'a man of honour', and his embrace of Chief Buthelezi despite the appalling toll of death his Inkatha movement had brought the ANC, had suddenly become the new orthodoxy for the ending of Africa's most bloody conflicts. The MPLA came under yet more pressure to follow the South African model – pressure already implicit in the Western diplomats' suggestion to head off the crisis in late September 1992 with the creation of a vice-presidency for Savimbi.

It was entirely consistent that in New York in mid-1993, after hearing a report from Mr Boutros Ghali that the situation was 'catastrophic', with over 1,000 people dying a day in Angola, the UN Security Council, while again condemning Unita for 'continuing military actions and repeated attempts to seize additional territory', still gave the rebels a three-month deadline to stop fighting before sanctions would be imposed. 'Time for another 100,000 people to be killed,' said one Western diplomat, appalled by the UN's failure to take concrete action against Unita. A Russian proposal to freeze Unita's overseas assets and its bank accounts was not accepted by the Western powers. Unita spokesmen were still able to travel freely on Côte D'Ivoire passports, lobbying vigorously against sanctions. Savimbi, meanwhile, was in frequent contact, by satellite telephone supplied by the Americans, with Mr Boutros Ghali and other long-standing friends and influential allies such as King Hassan and the Portuguese president Mario Soares.

As the UN deadline for sanctions came closer, Unita stepped up the eight-month siege of Cuito, moving columns of armoured cars from the border with Zaire to the edge of the town for a major assault and infiltrating men into the centre. The town was effectively partitioned, with all civilians in the government side – although this was a town which had voted for Unita in the 1992 elections. At the same time, for international consumption, the rebels announced a cease-fire on their clandestine radio. It was greeted with cautious reserve by both the government and the UN. Mr Beye, meanwhile, was trying to arrange a major summit of regional heads of state in Sao Tome or Gabon to which Savimbi was to come. A resumption of negotiations with President dos Santos would have obviated the need for sanctions. Mr Beye's famous optimism was on show again as he announced, 'within a few hours we will have a pleasant surprise for the people of Angola'. In New York the proposed UN arms and oil embargo against Unita was postponed for a week. But the Sao Tome summit never came off and in September 1993 partial UN sanctions to forbid the sale of weapons or fuel to Unita were finally imposed. General Ben Ben, Unita's Defence Chief, immediately boasted to Portuguese television that they would make no difference as Unita had weapons and ammunition for ten years. Whatever the stockpiles may have been, Unita was still able to use the great wealth of the diamond mines they had occupied since the election for military supplies from Eastern Europe and the Persian Gulf which continued in the final months of 1993 to come in to the Unita-controlled airfields of Huambo, Uige, Gove, Negage, and Jamba in the far south, via Zaire, unhindered by the sanctions. Just two days after the sanctions were imposed their impotence was exposed when a supply ship for Unita docked at Matadi port, a long-time Unita supply point in Zaire. No one even denounced it.

However, by September 1993 a new phase was emerging on the battlefield with a perceptible change in the balance of forces following a government offensive which had begun two months before. The rebuilding of the new national army, the FAA, under 38-year-old General Joao de Matos, was completed in record time and, with an extraordinary pragmatism, the FAA commanders had recruited former soldiers from the South African army with experience of fighting with Unita. The Pretoria security firm, Executive Outcomes, with equal pragmatism exchanged their contract with Unita for one with the government many of them had fought for so long. The sieges of Menongue, Luena, and Malange were partially lifted and Unita forces pushed far enough back to reopen the airports and fly in food and medical supplies to trapped civilians for the first time for six months.

The first aid agencies and UN personnel into the siege towns were overwhelmed by the scale of the needs which confronted them. 'The estimate of 1,000 deaths a day had clearly been very, very conservative,' said one World Food Programme official who was on some of the early flights. Fifty children a day, mostly from Malange, were flown back to Luanda's main hospital, Josina Machel. Half the patients died. Children were starving to death on the streets, mothers sold one of their children in the market to buy food for the others, families had been broken up with the adults lost or dead, homes were often flattened by the shelling, all possessions were lost, no one had been paid, and there were no resources with which to rebuild. Planting for a new agricultural season, even when people could summon the strength, was extremely dangerous because of the unmarked minefields which ringed the towns. A UN emergency humanitarian appeal for $226 million for Angola brought in just 40 per cent of what was needed.

By the following month the UN had brokered the latest of a complicated series of deals with Unita to give aid agencies access to civilians across the country on both sides of the lines, many of whom had seen no international aid for most of the year. The few aid agencies then working in Unita areas were reporting people dropping dead from starvation by the roadside. In government areas skeletal children crowded the soup kitchens and aid agencies had begun to open tented emergency feeding stations for tens of thousands of babies and small children. With the collapse of agriculture because of the fighting, the land mines cutting off vast areas, and the paralysis of all road transport, malnutrition was chronic everywhere. Not only was food scarce, but prices were soaring and wages often went unpaid, but were anyway unrealistically low. Even middle-class families were hungry.

The UN's new head of Humanitarian Affairs, Mozambican Manuel Aranda da Silva, persuaded all parties that humanitarian aid could no longer wait for the elusive political settlement between the government and Unita being sought at a new round of talks in the Zambian capital, Lusaka. As part of his successful deal, UN aid flights resumed into Unita's key towns of Huambo and Jamba, as well as the five besieged government towns: Malange, Luena, Menongue, Saurimo and Cuito. So dramatic was the situation in all these towns through the autumn that, in Malange for instance, the Catholic charity, Caritas, had 90 soup kitchens, and when the Irish charity Concern opened nine, each one was instantly over full with abandoned, malnourished children, some as young as two. Every relief flight bringing food and medicine in became an evacuation flight out with desperate people rioting on the airstrip for a place in the cargo plane, or even trying to cling to the wings and wheels as the pilot accelerated down the runway.

Cuito in particular became a showcase foreign aid operation. Unita controlled the road between the airport and the town and had an effective veto over who could enter or leave the town. No Angolans were allowed in or out, so no government capacity could be rebuilt. Da Silva worked hard to mobilise non-governmental organisations to go into Cuito to replace it. The siege was not over either for the 1,000 seriously wounded people initially identified by the UN as needing to be evacuated for treatment. Unita permission was never given, and aid workers said later they all died. With the new access agreement Unita was given control over 50 per cent of the food the UN brought into Cuito. The food for the government side was for the 50,000 or so civilians trapped in the town, while government soldiers continued to survive mainly on parachute drops. Unita, with no civilians in the part of the town under their control, brought peasants from many miles away to collect supplies under the eyes of television cameras and some UN supervision, but there was no doubt the major beneficiaries were the soldiers. Supplies of fuel to Unita were also carried in UN planes. 'It was certainly not a perfect arrangement, but it was the best we could do,' said da Silva.

By the autumn of 1993 the military tide was turning and Unita was slowly losing control of parts of the two thirds of the country it had held for most of the year. One of the first areas taken back by the government forces was the inland part of Benguela province and the all-important road which led from the coast to Huambo. The experiences of small towns like Cubal, retaken by the government army in late 1993, provided a terrible insight into Unita's mind-set. The population of this whole area, like those from Cubal, had had no firsthand experience of the earlier, South African-run, era of the war which had hit mainly the far south and the Central Highlands. All over the walls in Cubal was graffiti from before the 1992 elections. 'We don't want the MPLA', or, 'dos Santos finished', or 'Unita has won' gave a graphic indication of how the people of Cubal had felt about the election.

But nonetheless, when Unita took this town where it had many supporters, just weeks after the election, the soldiers went on a sacking and looting spree so destructive that the majority of people fled hundreds of miles through the rocks and bush to the safety of the ribbon of government control along the coast. 'People were burned alive in their huts. None of us will ever again be able to eat roast pork because the smell will be a memory of things too terrible for anyone to bear remembering – how could one black man do these things to another,' one former local official said.

The old and sick took refuge with the Spanish nuns in the Catholic mission hospital on the edge of the town's dirt airstrip. Through the nine months of Unita's occupation of the town they had made almost no contact with the nuns and never even brought their wounded to the mission. When Unita was driven out, the government troops found that every movable thing without exception had been taken from the town, including X-ray machines, surgical instruments, 78 of the 80 beds and the generator from the hospital, blackboards from the school walls, every piece of furniture from every house and shop. The bank was ransacked and all the money taken. The town generator was sabotaged and the hospital operating theatre, which had been the third most important of the province, had been used as a lavatory.

Cubal is almost surrounded by a wide river and land access to the town depends on bridges. Unita blew up the railway bridge completely and the main road bridge was impassable except to people on foot, with two great humps where the explosives had blown the bridge up off its base. Five bridges were destroyed and only the narrow bridge leading north, which the Unita troops had used for their flight, was intact.

Once Cubal was retaken, about half of its 200,000 people came back almost at once from the misery of the refugee camps outside Benguela where there had been no blankets, cooking pots, oil, soap or sugar. Those returning found their herds of cattle were long gone, a planting season missed, and that Cubal was an island of relative security with a small government defence force, but surrounded by countryside where Unita troops passed through often enough to mean the peasants dared not return to their villages, and that even nearby fields were dangerous. Every day new patients were brought into the mission hospital with mine injuries or bullet and machete wounds from Unita troops as near as five miles away. One man lying in the hospital had had his ears cut off, next to him lay a man with a dire head wound – he had been almost scalped. Often the injured were men trying in vain to restart work on their fields. The results of their not being able to farm the lush, rich land around the town were horribly visible. Under the trees outside the mission hospital more than 100 skeletal children lay with their mothers waiting for the twice daily feeding from the nuns.

The town had also become a magnet for newly displaced people from the next-door province of Huambo. There were 8,000 Ovimbundo peasants in a makeshift encampment just outside the town where two to four people were dying a day, mostly from hunger. The adults were in rags and the children naked, with scabies and kwashiokor visible everywhere. They had fled from Unita troops who, they said, kidnapped the men and boys, raped the women and girls, and stole the food from their homes. One of the *sobas* (village elders) spoke for the group: 'All our people voted for the peace, but the elections brought us only disaster and the loss of our land, livelihood, and many of our people.' The group, speaking Umbundo, then burst out all at once saying, 'we voted, but never again – the foreigners who came here and gave us elections made a big mistake – we never had fighting in our area before'. A tall gaunt woman drew nods of approval when she said 'we're Ovimbundos, but we don't understand why Savimbi says he's fighting for us. All it has meant to us is losing our homes and our children – they should take the arms away from people and let us have food again.'

One after another these refugees described the Unita troops coming into a village or a home and seeming to be mad, or drunk or drugged. Paulo Jorge, the Governor of Benguela province, described what he had seen in the frontline of the struggle for power in 1993 as 'a new kind of war for us, just terror and destruction, by units who are usually drugged, pushed on by the killings of those who fail or falter, and by the detention in Jamba of unknown hundreds or thousands of their family members'. The Unita bands which infiltrated Benguela called for 'the man with the dope' before they launched their attacks, and cocaine was often found in the pockets of dead Unita soldiers.

It was not until late 1994, with the retaking of Huambo in November by the government, that the picture drawn in Cubal could be clearly seen as a microcosm of what had happened across the country under Unita occupation. For those who remained behind

in Huambo once Unita took over in March 1993 it became 'a silent
town'. Under a regime of secret police, spies and denunciations,
people were afraid to talk, much less laugh. Even the foreign aid
agencies who worked there found they were completely under the
orders of Unita and had to accept any conditions Unita chose to
impose, such as where they could work, and even 'invitations' to
events such as marriages where Savimbi would be present.

One man described being arrested in Huambo in 1993 and
taken to a forced labour camp.

> People were rounded up because they were known to work for
> the government, certainly everyone who was known to be
> MPLA. Sometimes groups were taken off to the Sakaala forest
> and killed. Even before Unita had completely taken over the
> terror started after the election when Dr David Bernardino was
> killed. It was because he was independent and a socialist,
> everyone knew that from his work – it terrified people when he
> and Engineer Marcelino were killed, because if Unita dared kill
> them, who were known in the outside world, they could kill any
> of us.

He saw many of his friends die of hunger around him in his
detention camp. Corporal punishment and disappearances were
common. Fear was constant. Huambo mirrored the dictatorship
which Savimbi had established over nearly 20 years in Jamba.
Savimbi himself spent most of the time in a house he took over on
the beautiful tree-filled campus of the agricultural research institute
at Chianga, previously run by Dr Marcelino. Under the balcony a
great bunker deep enough for an armoured car was dug, hidden
by the shoulder-high grass.

But in November 1994 Savimbi was forced to retreat from
Huambo as the government forces closed in from the coast. As they
left, fleeing to the little town of Bailundo which was to be Savimbi's
next headquarters, the Unita troops systematically looted all the
foreign aid agencies' buildings, including the Red Cross complex
at Bomba Alta where all 56 foreign workers left in the town gathered
in the final days as the town changed hands. 'All of us lost every
single thing. They took all cars, radios, computers and
communications equipment,' said one official. It was a lesson to
the international community of Unita's ruthlessness, for once
turned on them, not Angolans.

The government retaking of Huambo came as, after a year of
talks in Lusaka, Unita was still refusing a cease-fire while holding
out for even more concessions in terms of ministries and provincial
governorships than had already been offered. The American officials
ever present behind the scenes in Lusaka tried to persuade the
Angolan government to stop their offensive short of Huambo,

saving face for Savimbi by leaving him in control of the ruined city when the cease-fire was signed. But, after a lengthy discussion in the MPLA Central Committee, the American plea was finally rejected and the military imperative of reasserting government control in Huambo accepted. However, the military leadership was overruled in their wish to continue the offensive in which the balance of forces had by then swung completely in their favour. The army commanders were then unanimous that they could have finished Unita militarily by pushing on to Bailundo, and thus finally forced an end to the unfulfilled commitments of Bicesse to return the whole country to government administration. They were overruled by the President, under tremendous pressure from the Americans and the United Nations to allow an outcome which would not be a defeat for Savimbi. The Lusaka Accords were signed in November 1944. There was to be a cease-fire, a new national army, and four ministries and seven vice-ministries for Unita. Savimbi himself was to have a 'special status' to be defined later. Lusaka was to be another peace agreement in which Unita was again, like Bicesse, treated as an equal partner, and in which there would be 'no winners, no losers'.

CHAPTER 7

The State Destroyed 1995–96

The entrance to the University faculty was deserted. In the wide hallway a pall of dust lay thick over the tiled floor and the wide staircase. A dark corridor, equally dusty, led off to the right, but at the end of it half a dozen yards of swept and washed corridor were dimly visible, an extraordinary sign of life in an apparently dead institution. Two doors leading off the clean part of the corridor were heavily padlocked and reinforced with steel. Inside one were two computers and printers, and the other housed a large refrigerator and shelves of seeds drying – a gene bank supported by Nordic aid money. There was one scientist, no students. One floor up there was another reinforced and padlocked door. Inside, one more scientist, with the only functioning telephone in the faculty and an embryonic computer network linking Angola to an e-mail circuit, though with regular electricity cuts in the capital its functioning was highly uncertain.

The dramatic situation of the University by the mid-1990s was a microcosm of Angola's loss of its skilled personnel and the collapse of state services across the board, from education and health to administration at local level. The economic paralysis of the long years of negotiations towards peace under UN auspices from early 1993 in Addis Ababa, Abidjan and then Lusaka had accelerated a trend of attrition which had for years seen the state slowly bled of talent and energy by the double curse of personal in-fighting of cliques in power and the erosion of the value of salaries. By the mid-1990s 20 years of building national capacity since independence from Portugal had been thrown away by a government unable to tackle the crisis of professional salaries which by then were approximately £15 a month for a university teacher, £2 for a civil servant and 63 pence for a nurse.

Four out of six faculties were closed down by mid-1995; 90 per cent of lecturers in some faculties were abroad on lucrative scholarships from which they were unlikely to return; Portuguese, Russian, Italian and Bulgarian teachers had been imported at salaries a hundred times bigger than their Angolan counterparts. The only Angolans still teaching were the most dedicated and resourceful, such as the two behind their steel doors in the deserted faculty. In addition they had simultaneously to do one or several other jobs, of which one at least needed to be paid in hard currency. In the health service, where the loss of intellectual capital was equally grave, the government brought in Korean and Vietnamese doctors who neither spoke their patients' language, nor had the working equipment or drugs to treat them. Leprosy, tuberculosis and sleeping sickness were epidemic across the northern provinces by mid-1995. One doctor described the health situation since 1993 as having gone from difficult to dangerous to dramatic.

The large provincial hospital in the northern town of Malange was typical of the conditions everywhere. The dark corridors were suffused with the suffocating smell of urine and infection. In the wards, men, women and children lay on beds which mostly had no mattresses. They were the victims of mine accidents, or suffering from TB, malaria, or malnutrition. Their relatives sat around their beds silently, fed them and waited for treatment that they knew only too well was unlikely to be possible.

Outside in the early morning highland mist four Vietnamese doctors in spotless white coats walked up the road to the hospital. The four women smiled and smiled politely as they described their working days in halting French. None of them spoke Portuguese. 'It is very very difficult. There are no medicines, and if we have to make an emergency operation the family must first find diesel in the market place so we can start the generator, then they must give the blood, and they will also have to look in the market for the drugs we need and buy them.' The Angolan doctor in charge of the hospital then arrived, also on foot, and said simply, 'it is not possible to describe what goes on here, only God can understand this suffering'.

Malange was one of the towns where the long drawn-out situation of no war, no peace, of the mid-1990s took the heaviest toll, with agricultural production at a very low level because of lack of access to most of the land. Unita held on to control of large parts of the province, which was on the traditional route to the diamond areas which were their financial lifeline, and to Zaire, their logistics lifeline. Most roads in the province were impassable because of sabotaged bridges or mines, though Norwegian People's Aid (NPA) had a team of 50 Angolan de-miners working to clear some agricultural land, where other aid agencies were starting vegetable growing, and the approaches to broken bridges on main roads once agreement was given by the military commanders of both sides in the area. To add to the province's difficulties, the Governor was best known as a big businessman with interests, in particular in the forestry which was one of the province's riches. The Governor's previous incarnation as Minister of Health had coincided with serious corruption scandals over medical supplies given by various donors. In the dark streets of Malange at night in 1996 the

Governor's house shone bright from his generator. Half a mile away one night our car headlights lit up a disused hall and dozens of small ragged boys ran out at the sound of the car engine to greet the young woman from one of the foreign aid agencies who had set up this child night shelter providing a meal and somewhere safe to sleep for Malange's many street boys. During the day dozens of these boys hung around the battered airstrip, racing on to the tarmac whenever a plane landed and picking up handfuls of grain or anything else which spilled from the cargo hold. Resourceful and energetic despite being stick thin from years of under-nourishment, they attached themselves briefly to anyone who might be a source of a few kwanzas or some food. These were the survivors of the hundreds of children who had become separated from their families during the long months of the Unita siege which began in 1993. Families had been broken up as mothers were killed or maimed in the desperate search for food which made them risk crossing the minefields which ringed the town. Some adults, abandoning their children, had fought their way onto the irregular cargo flights which brought in food from Luanda.

Hundreds of miles further south, Dondo, in Kwanza Norte province just 90 miles from Luanda, was another town where just one foreign woman aid worker struggled to hold back a tide of human misery where the government had long since given up. In the Portuguese colonial times this was a prosperous little town built around a wine factory. But by the mid-1990s the wine factory and the nearby clothing factory were closed. On the main square the pink and blue washed facades of the houses were crumbling and great trailing creepers hung off the iron balconies and clogged the verandas on the street. The last two hours of the road from Luanda was a jolting odyssey over vast red pot-holes in the road through thick forest. Monkeys jumped off the road and swung away into the darkness of the trees. With every mile clusters of fat tsetse flies on the car windscreen grew thicker. Just a few years before this province had been free of tsetse flies and the deadly sleeping sickness they carry. But the combination of Unita control over much of the province and over those further north, Uige and Zaire, where the flies bred along the River Kwanza, and the progressive collapse of state services in the areas controlled by the government, meant that the eradication programme was at a standstill. The result was villages and army camps along the river bank where 80 per cent of the population had the disease which is fatal if untreated. 'These villages will simply disappear by the end of the century,' said one doctor who had been through some of them for a survey made by the World Health Organisation.

Dondo's hospital was the magnet for peasants who got sleeping sickness and who could find a passing truck to bring them to it.

Perched up on a steep hill overlooking the town it was a classic crumbling Portuguese building. Outside it, and set at the bottom of the hill for the safety of those able to walk and who could have simply stepped off the steep hillside while in the trance of sleeping sickness, was a large emergency tent for the patients. Outside it the smoke of a hundred tiny cooking fires rose against the pale blue of an early morning sky as the families of the sick prepared their meals. The number of sleeping sickness patients had tripled between 1994 and 1995 and a hundred new patients were coming every month. A far greater number never made it to Dondo.

On the hospital veranda the patients from the tent sat or lay waiting for treatment. Their clothes were rags, none had shoes. Most showed the characteristic swollen faces of the disease, some walked about raving, a handful lay rigid with closed eyes and no amount of shaking would rouse them. Some also had malaria, others tuberculosis. The one doctor was a young Italian woman, Ada Merolle, working for NPA and treating only the sleeping sickness patients. NPA had built and equipped a small laboratory and paid for the Angolan technician who did the simple blood test which confirmed a sleeping sickness diagnosis. The very expensive arsenic-based drug for treatment was made in France and supplied by French aid, though Ada worried for how long that would go on. The Ministry of Health had no funds for the sleeping sickness programme, and indeed no drugs for the hospital at all. The only Angolan doctor in the town had not received his salary from the Ministry of Health for months and lived by taking private patients rather than by coming to the hospital. The inevitable four Vietnamese doctors, who looked after of the rest of the hospital, were sitting in their bare consulting room with no drugs, no equipment, and extremely minimal Portuguese to communicate with their patients. Two-year contracts in isolated Dondo with no family were, they said, much harder than they had expected. As a symbol of what had happened to Angola by the mid-1990s there was none more telling than this new epidemic of sleeping sickness down the dilapidated road which had cut Dondo off from the capital as effectively as though it were another country.

Far away in the Central Highlands, the town of Cuito was more like something from another continent and another age of warfare. Nothing could prepare you for the sight of the destruction of Cuito. The only parallels come from Europe's major wars: Stalingrad or Dresden. By 1996 the 15-month siege by Unita was two years past, but still the city was more rubble than buildings. On the main street, which was the frontline of the siege, blocks of flats had collapsed into heaps, the cathedral had only one wall and the bell tower standing, the pink shells of grandiose Portuguese government buildings were pocked with tens of thousands of bullet holes. Not a window, not a roof survived. The water system was destroyed and electricity had been only partially restored. The mass graves of the 30,000 people who died here in 1993–94 were hidden under pink, scarlet and orange flower beds in the central square. No one could go anywhere in the small town without passing the square and remembering the dead. In many homes family members were buried in their own little gardens and the memories of the dead were even closer in everyday comings and goings. The living carried a burden of experience which set them apart from anyone who did not live through that siege. Within an hour I met a man who had three times been in mine accidents and had lost one leg and an arm and a woman whose husband had been killed in the early days of the siege, whose child had died of starvation, whose second husband had been captured by Unita and never seen again, and who had then lost a leg in a mine accident. There are no words to convey the emotional desert these experiences have left for these individuals and their whole community to survive in.

But it is their impact on the next generation which will determine Angola's future. Antonio was a little six-year-old during the siege, which he spent cowering in the ruins of the town with several hundred other lost or orphaned children. By mid-1996 he was back in his village of Chipeta, 50 miles from Cuito, which had been occupied by Unita in 1993. He was leaning against the mud and wattle wall of his hut, in the shade, as we approached. He started and looked away. Then, as Evangelista, a senior social worker from the Cuito orphanage went up and touched his shoulder gently, he turned around, his face set and tears in his eyes. 'Saudades, saudades,' said Evangelista, meaning memories, nostalgia, sadness. After the cease-fire in late 1994 Antonio's family was traced to Chipeta, which had been abandoned by peasants on the run during Unita's major post-election offensive, but was returned to government control after the cease-fire. Antonio came home to this hut but found that his mother, father, brothers and sisters were all dead. His world had disappeared some time during the hours, days, weeks and months he sheltered in trenches and underground rooms from the relentless Unita artillery. Evangelista, who was with the children throughout the siege, was a kind and conscientious woman, but those days and months had exhausted her emotions to the core and her own grief for the dozen members of her immediate family who were killed seemed to have been put on hold lest it should overwhelm her. Antonio was beyond her responsibility now. He lived with his uncle, a skinny man with weary eyes who said that perhaps the boy was not feeling well and that there was little to eat and he was often too tired to go to school. Antonio had a piece of shrapnel lodged in his temple, visible as a jagged bump and almost certainly the source of his recurrent headaches.

Evangelista said she thought he needed an operation. But there was nothing she could do about it, Chipeta had no doctor or nurse, in Cuito the state hospital was on its knees and partially destroyed by some bad hits during the siege. A brand new plastic field hospital sent in as emergency aid from Italy was barely functioning, its Vietnamese and Angolan doctors without drugs or salaries here as everywhere else.

The considerable foreign interest in Cuito generated by the town's acute suffering had however brought in both funds and personnel for foreign-run projects. Cuito, and nearby Huambo, were the aid capitals for the 100 or so non-governmental organisations which had virtually replaced the government in social services. In marked contrast to the government-run side, one wing of Cuito's state hospital had been taken over, repainted and rehabilitated by Belgian Médicins Sans Frontières (MSF). Over 100 seriously ill children lay two to a bed, tended by one Angolan doctor with eight young Belgian doctors and nurses and a supply of drugs which would have been the envy of the state sector – all funded from Belgium. Outside the hospital, as in Dondo, stood an emergency tent. This time the emergency was not sleeping sickness, but malnutrition. In the tent and an improvised clinic in a hospital outbuilding 150 or more small children lay on straw matting with their mothers. Marasmus and kwashiokor were visible everywhere – reddish hair, protruding stomachs over little stick-like legs, or gaunt faces, skeletal frames and folds of skin which looked as though they could never fill out normally again. These children came both from the town of Cuito itself, illustrating the extreme difficulty vulnerable families were still having in making a living despite the end of the fighting, and from the Unita-controlled bush which stretched from a few miles outside the town to the horizon. From the air Bié province looked an empty wilderness of high pink grass and occasional clusters of trees. Only three roads were open because of the danger of mines and few outsiders knew anything of the conditions of civilians with Unita in this province. Judging by the children brought to MSF in Cuito's hospital, they were chronically poor and resourceless.

Just on the edge of the town was a place which told everything about the brutalising of Cuito. This place could not have existed in the Angola of the first decade of independence, the Angola of fierce pride in the dignity of its people, the Angola seen as a leader of the continent in its fight for real independence. A rough dirt road wound off the tarmac through scrubby grass to a cluster of tents – between them a scene of hell which even Dante could not have imagined. Outside one tent sat an old woman with no legs. Inside, in semi-darkness, other old women wearing thin rags were spreading bracken, grass and leaves for beds. It is bitter cold in the Central Highlands at night and these people had no coverings of any sort.

In the next tent another old woman was looking for something to wrap up a new born baby. There was no water to wash it. The camp had no water supply except the river a mile or so away, and few of those who had ended up here had the strength to walk that far. There was no medical attention and the new mother had seen no doctor or nurse during her pregnancy. She looked so thin and anaemic herself it was hard to imagine how she could feed the child. Two small children with the shrivelled skin of malnutrition were lying nearby alongside a woman who looked too weak to move. A young man with his legs crippled by polio, but with a handsome smiling face, crawled between the tents to beg for something to eat. A crowd of skinny, barely dressed children, shivering in the cold, pressed around us. Just beyond the tents a man missing one leg stood propped on his crutches in front of two dozen or so children. But this was not a makeshift school, a sign of a mutilated soldier's resourcefulness in this place without hope, instead the children were chanting the catechism and learning resignation to their terrible lot.

Suddenly a white truck with United Nations markings appeared jolting down the track from the airport road. Everyone, including old people and cripples who could barely crawl or swing themselves along on their hands, headed for the open space next to the camp's communal kitchen where the truck parked. Four young Brazilian soldiers jumped down. Tall, strong, in neatly pressed uniforms, they looked like creatures from another universe. In the back of their truck were two great vats of spaghetti soup, and as they opened them to pour the contents into the camp's own containers, clouds of steam and savoury smells of meat and vegetables spread over the silent crowd. The sun was starting to go down and a chill wind was getting up so that I wanted my jacket. The Brazilians, who said they brought this food once a week from their UN camp three miles away, jumped back into their truck and drove off in a haze of dust, orange against the setting sun. Then, to my stupefaction, the old women, the cripples and the children turned away from the hot food and began to crawl, limp and hop back to their tents. 'We can't eat the food unless the director is here, and that won't be until tomorrow,' said the old lady with no legs, inching towards her tent on her hands over the rough pathway. These people's utter deprivation was matched by their tragic resignation to being dehumanised.

Elsewhere in Cuito the Governor was talking about a mine clearance programme in a place where he wanted to start cross-country motorbike racing, the latest fad among the children of the privileged in Luanda. And in the aid agency offices young French soldiers from the UN's de-mining team played video games, others connected their lap-top computers to their offices in Europe or the US where they would soon return, or spoke to the their offices in

Luanda by radio or satellite telephone. Meanwhile reservoirs of water, electricity generators and daily UN flights to Luanda gave these foreigners lives of privilege inconceivable to Cuito's people.

The small perimeter of government control around Cuito, and the inaccessibility of the majority of the province, was typical of what was happening throughout the country. Anibal Rocha, then Minister of Territorial Administration, estimated in mid-1996 that 74 of 163 municipalities were occupied by Unita – including one provincial capital, Mbanza Congo in the north – and it controlled 264 of 398 communes. Unita thus controlled half the country (though much less than half the population) and gave no more sign of being prepared to give it up in accordance with the Lusaka agreement of November 1994 than they had in accordance with the Bicesse agreement four and a half years earlier.

The effects of the lack of freedom of movement because of military checkpoints and the effective partition of the country into two control zones was devastating to the agricultural economy of the peasants in the countryside, and contributed to the high prices which had brought the urban population to unprecedented expressions of social discontent. 'You have to question whether Unita really want to go along with this process – they're always ready with a new obstacle, and why have they prevented freedom of movement?' asked Peter Simpkin, then Head of the UN Emergency Office. One answer to his question came in May 1996 when an unusual rash of leaflets appeared in Luanda denouncing the government's inability to provide a living wage, water, electricity, education or healthcare, and calling for peaceful demonstrations. In this tightly controlled society such a thing was unimaginable, and shock waves went through Luanda. The authorities reacted immediately and the call for a demonstration was denounced on the radio. On the day no one turned out and no demonstration took place. The author of one of the pamphlets, who openly walked about showing them on the street, was arrested. He was not an Angolan, but a German priest called Konrad Liebsher whose nickname was 'The Beard', referring to his John the Baptist style appearance. Other foreign priests, working like him in Luanda's slums, appeared in court as witnesses for Liebsher, and said that they considered him rather moderate in his description of the current realities. The Angolan church leadership backed him too. Father Horatio, an Argentinian priest who had worked for years with street children in the capital, said that he sometimes felt so outraged by the state of the children who he found on the streets that he would take one who was starving or had open wounds and put him down outside the Palace of Congress if there was a meeting of the leadership of Party or government there, or even outside the President's home at Futungo.

The shanty towns ringing the capital had swollen to around three million people – a quarter of Angola's population – living in sub-human conditions. The comparison with Latin American squatter settlements was made by many, and Angola was increasingly being described as Africa's Brazil. The ostentatious luxury of the cars, houses, foreign healthcare and education of the nomenklatura had never been so evident and so bitterly discussed by those outside that magic circle. The respected Minister of Planning at the time, Pedro de Morais, made no attempt to put any kind of positive gloss on the situation. 'This is the most sombre phase of our economic history. Never have we seen such brutal problems: between the 5 per cent and 10 per cent of the very rich, and the rest who have nothing at all, there is an accelerating gap – it's unsustainable.' Mr de Morais denounced 'the lack of consistency and coherence in carrying out economic programmes' which had led to the final demoralisation of the middle ranks of the administration who had gone to jobs in the private sector leaving the Ministries stripped of the majority of their competent trained cadres. One former senior official described how 'in ten years the Heads of Departments and Directors of the Ministries have all disappeared, now the foreign businessmen who arrive wanting contracts see the Minister himself or the President to cut their deals'. One banker described the chaotic scramble for wealth as the end of an era. 'Everyone sees this can't continue.'

Institutionalised corruption and weighty vested interests were untouchable however. Oil, the main foreign exchange resource, was earning $10 million a day, but much of that never appeared in the national budget, going instead straight into foreign bank accounts. A two tier foreign exchange rate – with 80,000 kwanzas to the dollar at the official rate available to those favoured by the regime, or an unofficial rate of 240,000 kwanzas for everyone else – was one of the motors of corruption. Fortunes were made buying at one rate and selling at the other. The unofficial dollar rate rose by the day as businessmen paid above it for dollar cheques banked outside the country. Inflation soared to an estimated annual rate of over 3,000 per cent. In the legal foreign exchange shops dollars exchanged in the morning would no longer get the same rate in the afternoon of the same day. In one two-week period in May 1996 the rate soared from 150,000 to the dollar to 240,000.

So desperate had the struggle to survive become that morality was eroded even in the professions built on morality and altruism. A nurse would let a child with meningitis die, keeping the prescribed drug to sell in the market so that she could feed her own child rather than let him starve on what her salary could buy. A child referred for a blood transfusion by a doctor could be turned away by the nurse administering the transfusions because the child, or its family, had no bribe to pay her.

The social tension, with its clear message to Unita that its delaying tactics were succeeding in bringing the country to the brink of an urban explosion, triggered the sacking of the Prime Minister, the entire government, and the central bank governor in May 1996. The President went on television and gave a speech describing with unprecedented frankness just how bad the situation was, and announcing the cancellation of an official visit by him to Japan. 'We face total social degradation ... salaries have become merely symbolic ... the state system of health and education is virtually non-existent ... unemployment is soaring ... the infrastructure of electricity and water is close to paralysis and extremely degraded,' he said. The media was saturated with appeals for belt-tightening, more competent administrators and an understanding that, as for the previous two decades, the root cause of the misery was the long war.

But there were new dynamics. The Lusaka Accords' cease-fire had essentially frozen the status quo of a partition of the country since late 1994. It was a partition which had been accepted as a transitional device by the government in the context of Unita's political agreement to form the new national army, to take up the posts of four Ministers, seven Vice-Ministers, various provincial governors and ambassadors, and to have the 70 parliamentary deputies who won seats in the 1992 elections but never took them up, return to Luanda to do so. But with no progress on the political front the de facto partition had dramatic economic, political and military consequences especially because of Unita's control over a large proportion of the diamond areas taken in the new war of late 1992–93. Unita's diamond-for-arms trade was estimated by mid-1996 as worth $1 million a day, flown out to Zaire from the airports under Unita control such as Andulo, Bailundo and Negage, despite the UN presence in those places. The government was estimated to control less than one eighth of annual diamond sales, around $150 million worth. Every month's delay in completing the peace process and handing all territory back to the government was worth millions of dollars to Unita, allowing Savimbi to continue to import arms and to keep a military option in play in parallel with negotiations.

Throughout 1996, 40,000 to 60,000 Unita men and boys were assembled in camps across the country under UN auspices where they were to be disarmed and demobilised as part of the process of forming the single army designed by the Lusaka Accords of 1994 as it had been by Bicesse in 1991. This vital part of the peace process was as fraught the second time round as it had been the first in 1992. From the moment in January 1995 when the first 17,000 came in, it was clear that Unita had found a way to play with the Accords. Not only was the quartering very slow, but an extraordinary number of those who reported to the Quartering Areas had no arms to hand in and what they had did not include heavy or sophisticated weapons, nor munitions or logistics material. 'It is clear we do not have the best troops in the QAs; it is clear we do not have the best weapons in the QAs; it is clear we have no ammunition and war stores such as communications equipment and explosives,' said General Philip Sibanda, the quietly spoken, highly respected Zimbabwean UN military commander, in mid-1996. In addition, as time went on and UN personnel and aid agencies working in the camps had a chance to study the men over a period, they concluded that somewhere between 50 and 80 per cent were not in fact soldiers, but peasants who had been recently kidnapped and driven into the QAs by Unita to swell the numbers. Even Beye, who spent months publicly minimising the importance of these problems, was ready to show open irritation by August 1996. 'Where are the 3,000 soldiers who should be in the QAs – Unita could have brought them in in two days? Where are the 10,000 missing men? Where are the heavy weapons? Why are the senior officers not already in the FAA?' he asked. Savimbi had made personal promises to the Americans that all the men would be in QAs and all heavy weapons surrendered by 15 June 1996, but this, like so many of his previous promises, turned out to mean nothing.

The QAs were run by Unita, with a camp of UN soldiers nearby but not aiming to be in control, and another adjoining camp of UN civilians and foreign aid personnel in charge of civic education, health and food distribution. A mile or so outside the main camp, on a site usually chosen for its access to water and shade, UN tents were put up for those families which had come with the men. Skinny children and underfed mothers peopled these places, their physical state and low energy telling the story of their lives in the bush in Unita controlled areas. The World Food Programme ran supplementary feeding programmes in almost all the demobilisation camps. The QAs themselves were bleak and frightening places. Unita discipline was harsh, with casual brutality, corporal punishment and summary executions reported by UN personnel working with them. Desertions from the QAs ran into thousands, and confusion perennially surrounded the figures as aid agencies tried to log numbers of child soldiers and found not only that their names and ages changed between interviews, but that often they would simply disappear and a vague explanation that they had gone to visit their families would only add to the muddle.

In Negage in the northern Highlands, once the government's main air base but taken by Unita in one of the most bitter and hard fought engagements of the post-election war, the UN troops at the QA were an impeccably efficient Indian company. Their commander had good relations on a daily basis with the Unita colonel in charge of 5,000 men and boys, but had noticed something about him he found very hard to understand: the Unita colonel constantly changed his story about who he was and where he came from, even how old he was and how long he had been in Unita. UN civilian workers in the camp, there to teach civic education to prepare the men for a return to civilian life which in many cases they had never known, noted the same thing. 'These men lie all the time, even about the most trivial things which could not possibly matter,' said one. Sudden temper tantrums and a 90 per cent illiteracy rate were also noted. The years of isolation in the bush, the violent circumstances in which so many had been inducted into Unita and the totalitarian nature of the organisation had produced people whose conformity to the group was a source of astonishment to the well-educated and thoughtful Indians. Asked what they would like to do after demobilisation the young boys playing cards outside their tent gave the same answer as their colonel had given an hour before: 'If I am ordered to demobilise I will do it, if I am ordered to go to the countryside or to Luanda I will do it, if I am ordered to remain in the army I will do it.'

Such mental attitudes were hardly auspicious for the creation of the Lusaka Accords' linchpin, the new single national army, nor for tens of thousands of men to return to the hard self-sufficiency of peasant life, especially in a country so devastated that all normal patterns of production, supply and distribution were broken and would have to be patiently rebuilt.

It was the government military, the FAA, knowing from experience a good deal about these men who had been their enemies, and in some cases their brother soldiers, which brought the most imagination to bear on the problem of the ex-soldiers' future. The FAA prepared a plan which called for a Fourth Branch of the army to incorporate all those soldiers from both Unita and FAA not chosen for the new 90,000 strong military, in brigades for reconstruction of the country's infrastructure. During their two years in the Fourth Branch these 100,000 men would learn a skill, such as building, be given land to build a house, and have a guarantee from the military that they would buy the first year's harvest. From his experience after Zimbabwe's war of independence the UN's General Sibanda was a supporter of the idea: 'They need an organisation to look after them for several years, demobilisation straight from the QAs is definitely not a good idea judging by our experience, it almost created a disaster for us.' Similarly Mozambique's leaders warned of the chaos that had marked the demobilisation straight from the camps of their own Frelimo and Renamo soldiers. But the FAA's proposal would have cost an estimated $800 million and was promptly turned down by the international community which put forward alternative plans costing ten times less. Government ministers too rejected the idea as giving power to the military which they believed should have been wielded by the government itself – preferring to ignore the lack of government capacity which the President himself had so graphically described. The UN and donor-backed suggestion was, as in Mozambique, to give each soldier a farming kit, six months' money, and transport to wherever he wanted to settle down. General Joao de Matos, Angola's chief of staff was typically forthright about the likely consequences:

> Personally I think a soldier after 12–15 years in the army is not a farm worker – the only thing he knows is war. He'll immediately sell the kit and spend the money, waste it ... he has no experience of economy or organisation and in two weeks he's a potential bandit. In contrast our programme would mean that for four years he'll obey military orders, get paid, get fed, have health and education support, with a guarantee of a house and land which will belong to him. We have a chance with our programme of transforming soldiers into civilians and of guaranteeing the stability of Angola. Without it the FAA will have a lot of work to do to maintain stability.

In early June 1996 the first 15 officers from Unita finally came to Luanda for incorporation into the FAA and General Matos laid down a deadline for the new army to then be completed in two months. He was making a political point with this ambitious timetable, aiming to end the long debilitating stalemate of neither war nor peace. 'At that point, with a unified army, the state administration will be restored over the whole country. We are tired of this peace process, it's been going on too long. The country is in a morass, the people are exhausted, the international community has had enough. So much money has been wasted.' With the creation of the unified army, the technical end of the peace process would be certified by the UN, which could then leave. At that point all those Unita soldiers outside the FAA and defending Unita areas would be rebels and liable to attack by the government army thus freed of the constraints put on them by the cease-fire imposed by the international community since the Lusaka Accords 20 months before. But predictably the deadline came and went, ignored by Unita.

General Matos was alone among top officials in stating so openly that the stalemate could not be allowed to continue under the supervision of a UN which, he said, could never really monitor what Unita was doing. 'They cannot work out what is really happening in Unita areas, or where the troops or weapon stocks are. They have to ask for Unita permission to go anywhere in their zone and, in any case, Unita's hidden zones have very difficult access.' From the military point of view 1995–96 were highly dangerous years despite the successful rebuilding of the FAA. Unita was constantly rearming with weapons flown in from Zaire, and General Matos' own troops in the FAA were suffering, like everyone else, from the economic crisis and, in addition, from the frustration of life confined to barracks although they suspected the war was not over.

It was not only militarily that the UN and the international community could not work out what Unita was doing. The US ambassador, who was a frequent visitor to the Unita leader in Bailundo, was given four different versions of Savimbi's plans to accept or not accept the vice-presidency which became one of the touchstones of his changing moods in 1996. The offer of one of two vice-presidencies had been made to Savimbi by President dos Santos personally – it was not in the Lusaka Accords which had merely offered him a 'special status'. Not until Unita's Extraordinary Congress in Bailundo on 3 August 1996 was the vice-presidency categorically rejected, to the stupefaction of both government and the UN. Months before, two houses had been prepared for Savimbi in Luanda by the government and Ministers were confidently predicting, from their own meetings with him, that he would arrive in the capital by June, or at least by September. At four summits between the two leaders Savimbi promised, on various occasions, to have the new army and the government of national unity and reconciliation in place by July and to take any position offered him by dos Santos, who he again referred to as 'my President' as he had when the two appeared together at the donors' conference in Brussels the previous year. The fact that the four summits were all held outside Angola at Savimbi's insistence did not ring sufficient warning bells with the international community, though most Angolans became increasingly pessimistic about Unita's intentions. A very bellicose speech from Savimbi on 13 March totally contradicted all the positive public assurances, but as usual was virtually ignored as a political signal, except by Angolans. For Maitre Beye, for instance, it was positive enough that the two leaders were meeting and talking, and if the results were slow in coming that was only to be expected in the aftermath of such a long war where bitterness and mistrust bedevilled every attempt to move forward. The Alice in Wonderland quality of the period was encapsulated in the 8 May passing of a revision of the Amnesty law which had actually been drafted by Unita. Dozens of MPLA parliamentarians spoke against it, but in the end it was passed under strong pressure from the President, with the parliamentarians maintaining the MPLA's culture of consensus.

The summits between the two leaders were one of the clearest signs of the most fundamental political change which had taken place over the last decade – the transformation of Angola from the MPLA's one-party state, not to a multi-party state, but to a presidential regime. So the most delicate and dangerous period of Angola's post-independence history was in the hands of one man. In the meetings between President dos Santos and Savimbi no one knew what passed between the two men, what threats or promises were made by one or the other. One US diplomat crudely summed up the situation his country had done so much to create, by saying 'the Party, the Parliament, the Council of Ministers, are all out of power now, all dos Santos has to contend with is keeping the military sweet'. The military – the FAA – was indeed a new phenomenon in post-independence Angola – a military force independent of the politicians, in marked contrast to the highly politicised FAPLA, the MPLA's army since the liberation struggle. For Angola's civilian political class their new situation of virtual impotence was a mark of shame. As the MPLA had lost its physical capacity to govern or to take care of people so noticeably in the provinces, so in the capital had its cadres lost the confidence of being the country's leadership. The lawyers and economists who in the mid-1980s had still been the backbone of a party which prided itself on a history of discipline, debate, and consensus, had by the mid-1990s shifted their priorities to private life: their own businesses, children at schools in South Africa or Portugal.

In December 1995, in a gesture towards Washington which only a presidential regime could have made, Angola failed to vote in the annual United Nations General Assembly debate against the US blockade of Cuba. It was a gesture so heavy with political symbolism of the new political era that shock waves reverberated through Luanda. Many of those who heard it could not believe it was true and that the years of shared history and shared sacrifice with the Cubans could have been thus repudiated. The shame and anger felt by those who had fought with the Cubans over the years was beyond description, and the Cuban ambassador was overwhelmed by personal apologies. Fidel Castro did not wait long to send two well-known generals from Havana to tell President dos Santos personally how furious he was.

But the death of principle and idealism was not everywhere. The MPLA party building was a tower block next to the radio and television stations on the heights of Luanda above the bay and the steamy streets at sea level. Once it was the centrepiece of the one-party state and, from the tight security at first the gate and then the reception desk to the icy cold air-conditioned waiting rooms full of people prepared to wait as long as it took, the sense of power was palpable. But that was in another time, before the coming of multi-party politics as part of the price for ending the war with the Bicesse agreement of 1991. In 1996, with no state funding for the Party and no more Party cells in the workplace, the marble entrance hall was empty, you could walk up flights of stairs, down long silent corridors and find no one. Only on the ground floor, through two sets of great glass doors, did the Party come alive – in its international department. Secretaries made appointments, the fax machine clicked, the telephone rang. Paulo Jorge, MPLA International Secretary and still a member of the Political Bureau, was busy every hour of the day with a procession of foreign visitors, from old friends, such as China and Vietnam, representing parties which still called themselves fraternal, to the American ambassador, the first in Angola after 20 years of diplomatic frost from Washington. Paulo Jorge, sipping delicate lemon grass tea picked from his garden, wearing the same worn safari suits which in the post-independence era were the trademark of new-style African leaders like Julius Nyerere and Kenneth Kaunda, described himself as 'the Don Quixote of the country'. He pointed to the government decree of 1992 which allowed ministers to become businessmen. 'That brought a change in mentality – moral values disappeared, replaced by material values.' He joked about the people who told him he was foolish not to go into business like everyone else and who thus showed how completely they had missed the point of this man's life. Extraordinarily, he was utterly unembittered by the knowledge of what he had lost.

The people of Angola, such as those in the ruined towns of Cuito and Malange, or the university students with no faculty to study in, or the street children robbed of a childhood, have paid a high price for the destruction of the political dreams of men like Paulo Jorge and Lucio Lara, David Bernardino and the Marcelinos. Unita, the apartheid leaders of South Africa, and Washington with its Cold War dogmatism were the greatest destroyers, but there were others too, much closer to home. The first President of Angola, the doctor and poet Agostinho Neto, used to say that the goal of the MPLA was simply to be able to solve the people's problems: 'resoudre les problems du peuple.' Years later Lucio Lara was to say sadly

I don't have illusions about many things any more. In the Angolan struggle perhaps we didn't have philosophers or sociologists, but we had those words of Neto's, 'the most important thing is to solve the people's problems'. Once in the Council of Ministers I heard someone say that we should stop using this phrase. I thought then maybe he was right, because no one spoke out against him. In my opinion this was when the Party began to collapse. The leaders felt they all had the right to be rich. That was the beginning of the destruction of our life.

The Kabila Factor 1997

On 6 April 1994 the presidential plane carrying Rwanda's leader, Juvenal Habyarimana, back from a regional summit in Tanzania was hit by two missiles just before landing and crashed, killing all on board. The plane crash was the signal for Hutu extremists, who feared the democratisation plan which the late president had reluctantly agreed to under regional pressure, to unleash a planned genocide of Rwanda's Tutsi minority. The plotters, from the elite 1,500 strong Presidential Guard and some elements of the army, threw up road blocks in the capital Kigali, and began house to house searches for their victims. Working from long lists, they killed first the Prime Minister Agathe Uwilingiyimana, the President of the Constitutional Court, Joseph Kavaruganda, and dozens of liberal politicians or democrats who had been in favour of the regional plan to end Rwanda's long cycle of ethnic pogroms by sharing power with Tutsis. People were killed in their thousands and tens of thousands because they were Tutsis, because they were members of Hutu opposition parties which were in favour of power-sharing, because they tried, as many priests and nuns did, to stop militiamen from killing others, or simply because they were well-dressed, spoke good French and were clearly from the most privileged section of society. The Interahamwe, the militia born in the youth movement of the ruling party, who did most of the killing, were mostly recruited among the poorer sections of society, and they in turn drew to them crowds of street boys and the homeless unemployed. By the day after the plane crash the killing had spread to the interior of the country and was organised by local civil servants and councillors (all members of the ruling party) who mobilised the local gendarmerie and Interahamwe, forced peasants to join in the killing and looting, and called on the army, the FAR, if there was resistance. Most of the victims were hacked to death with machetes and suffered slow and gruesome deaths. Manhunts, rape, disembowelling of pregnant women, killing of children, throwing people down wells, burning them alive in their homes, was the grim pattern everywhere. The mass killing went on through April and May and the dead were estimated as at least 850,000, 11 per cent of the population.

This genocide was the spark which was to transform Angola's political and military situation three years later.

The planners and perpetrators of the Rwandan genocide fled the country as the regime collapsed before the Tutsi-led Rwanda Patrotic Front (RPF). At least a million people crossed into eastern Zaire in mid-1994 and were installed in refugee camps under the auspices of the United Nations and other aid agencies. But these camps became the breeding camps of new plans of genocide by the Hutu extremist leaders, arms were bought in, and relations cultivated with the ill-disciplined soldiers of Mobutu Sese Seko, the FAZ. Hit and run raids back into Rwanda kept the country seriously destabilised and neighbouring Uganda too suffered a wave of destabilisation on the Western border as the FAZ and ex-FAR joined forces with Ugandan dissidents from the Idi Amin days led by Colonel Juma Oris, previously mainly active from Sudan into northern Uganda. Invasions were planned into both Rwanda and Burundi to exterminate the Tutsi minorities.

Eastern Zaire became a tinderbox waiting for the match. The FAZ traditionally made their living by the pillage of local peasants, and together they and the former FAR in their camps selected as a target prosperous Tutsi farmers who had moved from Rwanda into the emptier lands of eastern Zaire more than a generation before. But this group, the Banyamulenge, who bore a long-standing grudge against the regime in Kinshasa which had never given them citizenship, fought back for their land, and enlisted the help of a non-Tutsi Zairian from Shaba with a 30-year-long history of resistance to Mobutu – Laurent Kabila.

Kabila in seven months was to make a meteoric rise from a life in obscurity making a living as a businessman between Zaire and Tanzania after the failure of the first revolt against Mobutu in the 1960s when Che Guevara and his handful of Cuban fighters withdrew ignominiously. President Yoweri Museveni of Uganda and former president Julius Nyerere of Tanzania were the key people in the region to see Kabila as the man history was waiting for.

The combination of circumstances of the destabilisation of Uganda; the regional trauma caused by the Rwandan genocide and the very real possibility that it could be repeated by the same people who had created armed virtual mini-states inside their refugee camps in Zaire and Tanzania; and the personalities of Museveni and General Paul Kagame, Vice-President of Rwanda and once a trusted military officer in Museveni's army, opened the door to dramatic action. New geo-politics since the end of the Cold War meant that the US had no taste for intervention in Zaire themselves, but were only too happy to see others pre-empt a French one, and indeed gave tacit support to the Ugandan and Rwandan leaders.

These two proud and self-confident men had each their own
history of successfully taking military action against all the odds to
rescue their countries from the leadership of debased, corrupt
cliques whose power was based on exploitation of ethnicity.
Museveni started a guerrilla war in 1979 with a handful of men
and only the supplies they managed to capture from the regime.
No one believed he could possibly build from that humble start
the people's army which eventually forced Milton Obote and then
his military successor, Tito Okello, out of power. Kagame's RPF
guerrillas similarly confronted a strong and militarised state with
major international backing from both France and Belgium. Close
to both men, both in personal style and in life experience, was the
Eritrean leader, Issias Aferworki, who brought his country to
independence after a 30-year war against an Ethiopian army which
was one of the largest and best-equipped in Africa. Eritrea too in
the early 1990s was the victim of low-level destabilisation engineered
by Sudan, like Uganda's northern war, and both countries were
supporting rebels fighting the obscurantist Islamist regime in
Khartoum. The fourth part of the regional jigsaw was the Angolan
military, out of patience with the flagrant flouting of the international
community by the Angolan rebel movement, Unita, for whom
Zaire was still the crucial supply and logistics line and continuing
diplomatic support mechanism as it had been through the long years
of US backing through the Cold War.

Mobutu's illness was also a factor in the decision to move.
Worsening prostate cancer and months spent abroad meant the
Zairian leader had ceased to govern his vast crumbling domain, and
since it had lost its strategic value to the US with the end of the
Cold War the Zairian state had become a house of cards waiting
for someone to blow it over. Kabila turned out to be the man.

In October 1996, two years of the abusive use of the Zairian
camps by the masters of the genocide, and the utter failure of the
international community to make the UN Tribunal in Arusha a
credible player in exposing and punishing those guilty of the
genocide, had brought the regional leaders to the point where they
were ready for action on their own terms. War began in South Kivu
in October when the FAZ and ex-FAR attacked Tutsi farmers.
On 18 October four Zairian political groups came together in
Memera, South Kivu, and formed the Alliance of Democratic
Forces for Liberation (AFDL). Laurent Kabila's Revolutionary
Party of the People (PRP) was the only one of the four with no
troops, but what he did have was a political programme and the
legitimacy of his long struggle, including recent years when the
PRP tried to run a socialist programme in their Hewa Bora (Our
Land) area, virtually a liberated territory where there was no
government presence.

The porous nature of the frontiers in the region, and the Tutsi diaspora which was the result of so many waves of ethnic persecution, had produced within the Rwandan military a hard-core of exceptionally well-trained soldiers whose self-definition was as Zairians. Around this core new units were trained as fast as volunteers presented themselves. Rwandan and Ugandan logistics and supplies were made available. Meanwhile, the international community tried, under French and Canadian leadership to put a military force into eastern Zaire as a buffer which would have effectively protected the ex-FAR and the refugees they controlled from the retribution which was clearly coming from the local population and from the Rwandan military. But a rapid military strike at the camps by the RPF and Kabila's men pre-empted the ill-conceived international initiative ever getting beyond the planning stage, and hundreds of thousands of refugees walked back into Rwanda of their own free will. The leaders of the genocide were not among them, they fled again further west, driving tens of thousands of women and children along with them into the forests of Zaire.

The breaking of the camps sharply changed the balance of forces regionally, though when Kabila was first quoted in the eastern Zairian town of Goma as saying he intended nothing less than the overthrow of Mobutu in Kinshasa, few believed he had a chance of doing so. However, his troops showed an extraordinary resilience and discipline and were able to march 40 to 60 miles a day. Mobutu's army showed no inclination to fight in the early weeks, and many of his soldiers changed sides. By the end of the year the President prepared to return home from his stay in France and Switzerland and asked his old ally Jonas Savimbi for the use of Unita units to hold back the rebels in certain areas, notably round his palace in Gbadolite in the north of the country. These were troops which should have been already demobilised months before by the UN and whose use in Zaire's civil war was to prove fatal to Mobutu as it brought Angola decisively into the coalition of forces fighting for his overthrow.

In February the balance of forces swung further in favour of Kabila when several thousand men from the families of former Katangese gendarmes who had been in exile in Angola since the 1960s were flown from Luanda to Tanzania, then to Rwanda and then to Bukavu in eastern Zaire. These units first joined Kabila's war when they fought in Kisangani which the regime tried to hold with mercenaries of various European nationalities. The Katangese impact was decisive. The Angolan military provided equipment and, most importantly, the key transport and logistics for the lightening campaign which then brought the mining capital of Lubumbashi, and the capital Kinshasa itself, into Kabila's hands after a seven-month campaign in which his men had walked across a country the size of Western Europe.

For Jonas Savimbi the fall of Mobutu was a dramatic set-back he could never recover from. It left him without the rear base which had served as the all-important conduit for the illegal diamond sales which financed his war, as the entry point for his equipment, and as the way in and out from his headquarters in Bailundo. For the first time for 30 years he was isolated. His allies over the years – Portuguese, South Africans, Americans – had left him at different times, but he had always found a way to carry on his destruction of his country, through Zaire and with the tacit support of Africa's other dinosaur leaders – from Morocco, Kenya, Côte D'Ivoire, Togo and Gabon. The loss of Mobutu faced him with a completely new situation – militarily, logistically and politically for the long term. In the short term his units, which were defeated in Zaire during the war which transformed it into Congo, retreated over the border into Congo/Brazzaville and thence back into the diamond areas of Angola, still not under government control. But Savimbi's isolation grew even deeper. The ripples of Kabila's triumph spread to neighbouring Congo/Brazzaville and another Savimbi ally, President Pascal Lissouba, was soon fighting for his political life.

All over Africa the end of Mobutu was felt as the beginning of the end of an era. A handful of African leaders had decided that the continent's people deserved to see an alliance of corrupt and brutal tyrants finally meet justice, and had successfully seen through a stunningly bold military campaign. The popular mood in many other countries saw their own dinosaurs as soon to go too.

For Angola the impact of the Kabila factor offered a promise even more profound in the long term than its immediate narrowing of Savimbi's choices. The new politics of the regional leadership had everything in common with the old lost aspirations of 1975 and could have been encapsulated in Neto's simple dream of, 'solving the people's problems'. The Frontline States, like Angola, which had provided the continent's political leadership for the long years of the fight against apartheid, but paid too heavy a price to sustain that leadership, saw the baton pass to a new confident generation in Central Africa. These men's great advantage would be that their political choices at home would be free from sabotage by powerful outsiders whose priorities were set by the Cold War, and by the desire to prop up a white minority government in Pretoria.

Characters

MPLA

President Jose Eduardo dos Santos.

Lucio Lara, founding member of the MPLA, Organising Secretary of the Party, Political Bureau member, leader of the National Assembly, elected member of Parliament.

Paulo Jorge, Foreign Minister, Governor of Benguela province, MPLA International Secretary, Political Bureau member.

Lopo de Nascimento, first Prime Minister of independent Angola, Governor of Huila province, Minister of Territorial Administration to May 1992, Political Bureau member.

General Joao de Matos, Chief of General Staff of FAA December 1992.

UN

Margaret Anstee, Special Representative of UN Secretary-General 1992–93.

Alioune Blondin Beye, Special Representative of UN Secretary-General 1993– .

Marrack Goulding, former British ambassador to Angola, UN Under-Secretary-General in Peace Keeping and then Political Affairs.

General Philip Sibanda, (Zimbabwe) UN Military Chief in Angola.

Manuel Aranda da Silva, Director of Humanitarian Coordination Unit.

Philippe Borel, Representative of World Food Programme.

Unita

Jonas Savimbi.

Elias Salupeto Pena, nephew of Savimbi and head of Unita delegation to the Joint Political and Military Commission.

General Ben Ben, nephew of Savimbi and Chief of General Staff

Abel Chivukuvuku, Unita 'Foreign Minister'.

General Eugenio Manuvakola, Secretary-General of Unita and leader of Unita delegation in negotiations in Addis Ababa and thereafter 1993 signatory of The Lusaka Protocol 1994.

Antonio da Costa Fernandes, 'Foreign Minister' until he defected, February 1992.

Miguel Nzau Puna, 'Interior Minister', defected February 1992.

Wilson dos Santos, killed 1991.

Tito Chingunji, killed late 1991.

Bibliography

Anstee, M.J. (1996) *Orphan of the Cold War* (Basingstoke: Macmillan).

Antunes, A.L. (1979) *South of Nowhere* (London: Chatto and Windus).

Bridgland, F. (1986) *Jonas Savimbi, A Key to Africa* (Edinburgh: Mainstream Publishing).

Crocker, C.A. (1993) *High Noon in Southern Africa: Making Peace in a Rough Neighbourhood* (New York: W.W. Norton).

Davidson, B. (1972) *In the Eye of the Storm: Angola's People* (New York: Doubleday).

Johnson, P. and Martin, D. (eds) (1989) *Front-line Southern Africa* (Peterborough: Ryan).

Minter, W. (1986) *King Soloman's Mines Revisited* (New York: Basic Books).

Minter, K. (1994) *Apartheid's Contras* (London: Zed Press).

Maier, K. (1996) *Angola: Promises and Lies* (London: Serif).

Pepetela (1983) *Mayombe* (London: Heinemann).

Wolfers, M. and Bergerol, J. (1983) *Angola in the Front Line* (London: Zed Press).

Wright, G. (1996) *The Destruction of a Nation* (London: Pluto Press).

Index

diamonds 2, 4
  for arms 67, 74, 81, 89
  mines occupied 67, 68, 74
  seized by Unita 29
de Nascimento, Lopo 51, 53, 57
dos Santos, General Antonio
  (Ndalu) 39
dos Santos, President Jose
  Eduardo 40, 60, 62, 71
  meets Gorbachev 29
  meets Savimbi 42, 44, 93–4
dos Santos, Onofre 53, 56
dos Santos, Wilson 47
Du Toit, Winan Petrus Johannes
  20–1, 28

education 80–1, 87, 89
elections 45, 48, 50–6
  results 56–60, 67–8
electricity supply 84, 87, 89
Executive Outcomes 68–9, 74

FAA (Angolan Armed Forces) 56,
  74, 90, 91–3, 94
  Fourth Branch 91–2
FAPLA (Popular Armed Forces
  for the Liberation of Angola
  (MPLA) 21, 27, 34, 35, 45,
  46
  demobilisation 54–5, 63
Fernandes, Antonio da Costa 10,
  49, 67
FLEC (Front for the Liberation
  of the Cabinda Enclave) 66
Flynn, John 50, 64
FNLA (National Front for the
  Liberation of Angola)
  mercenaries 5
  support from United States 1–2
  support from Zaire 2–3
Freira, Amilcar 28
French intelligence service 1, 11

Gbadolite agreement 42, 46
Georgiou, Costas (Colonel
  Callan) 5
Gorbachov, Mikael 29, 45
Goulding, Marrack 44, 66

Habyarimana, Juvenal 96

Hassan, King 73
health service xiii, xiv, 81–3, 85,
  87, 89
Houphouet-Boigny, President 71
Huambo xii–xiii, 7
  attacked 61–2, 68–9
  retaken by MPLA 77–9
Huila 13, 16, 48
human rights abuses
  by MPLA 65
  by South Africans 12
  by Unita 13–19, 41, 48–9, 58,
    76, 78

IMF (International Monetary
  Fund) 42
independence 1–2, 3–4

Jamba 11–12, 19, 38, 47–8, 51,
  52
Jorge, Paulo 26, 68, 77, 95
JPMC (Joint Political Military
  Commission) 45, 46, 48, 61,
  63

Kabila, Laurent 97, 98, 99
Kamina 38, 41
Kasrils, Ronnie 9
Kaunda, Kenneth 42
Kavaruganda, Joseph 96
Kennedy, Michael 56
kidnapping by Unita 11, 15–16,
  17, 29, 77
  of election officials 53, 58
Kissinger, Henry 2, 6
Kito, Rodrigues 31

Lara, Lucio xv, xvi, 3, 24, 26, 95
Lehrman, Lewis 23
Liebsher, Konrad 87
Lobito 7, 53, 54, 62
Low Intensity Conflict 13
Luanda xi–xii, 1, 2–3, 7–8
  fighting in 62–5
Lubango 3, 12, 16, 62
Luena 36, 52, 69, 71, 74, 75
Lumumba, Patrice 2
Lusaka Accords 79, 87, 89–90

Machel, Samora 30, 34

Index by Sue Carlton